Become a Vacation & Leisure Travel Agent

Become a Vacation & Leisure Travel Agent

By Anton Anderssen

Hartforth Publications

Copyright 2004
Hartforth Publications
No parts of this book may be reproduced in any form, or by any means, without the permission of the publisher. We prosecute! Published by

4177 Garrick Ave   Warren Michigan 48091
(586) 757 4177 Voice / (313) 557 6367 Fax
International Standard Book Number:
0 9666119 85
Printed in the United States
First Edition. Second Printing

Dedication

To Marco Airaghi

Love, Hugs, and Dreams

Anton Anderssen

CONTENTS.

About the Author.. 7
Acknowledgements.. 8
Foreword.. 9
Suppliers... 12
Booking... 16
Tax Advantages... 20
Las Vegas.. 30
Orlando... 47
Alaska.. 55
Car Rentals.. 56
Cruise Lines... 58
Tour Operators... 65
Passwords.. 72
Special Offer... 128

About the Author

Dr. Anton Anderssen earned a Juris Doctor degree from Wayne State University School of Law, and continued with coursework in Labor Law. He is a member of Mensa, the high IQ society, and several other high IQ groups including Triple 9 Society, ISPE, & Prometheus. He is a PADI certified open water scuba diver, has NASA moon rock certification, has studied 27 different languages, performs piano during the holiday season at venues such as the Detroit Institute of Arts, is legally titled in Great Britain as "The Lord of Hartforth," worked as a producer for the TV Show "Perspective on the Arts," develops adult enrichment classes for 20 public school districts and community colleges, has been a volunteer at Gilda's Club, The International Institute, American Red Cross, and Public Television, and has written several books and training manuals. He is the proprietor of Anton Anderssen Travel, and teaches travel industry classes at Washtenaw & Henry Ford Community Colleges.

Acknowledgments

I am grateful to Dr. Raymond Archer of Indiana University who taught me how to love books. He also taught me how to think, and how to experience life. He taught me French language and grammar. He taught my Freshman English class, and inspired me to write. He taught my comparative literature classes and introduced me to the world's greatest literature, the arts, and their inter-relationship. I owe my happiness to Professor Archer...he taught me how to find meaning in my life.

Foreword

Benefits of being in the Travel Industry

To become a travel agent is to become a new person! Everyone loves to meet interesting people, experience new and delicious cuisine, stroll down streets where the rich and famous have trod, smell exotic flowers growing naturally along winding paths, hearing the laughter of children as they meet Mickey Mouse for the first time, strolling along the deck of a cruise ship in the moonlight holding hands with someone you love. As a travel agent, you get paid to arrange for others to experience these exciting things, and when you do them yourself, you'll likely be paying a fraction of the cost, and writing off on your taxes whatever money you do spend! This is only the beginning. Travel agents are invited to promotional seminars sponsored by the suppliers....maybe gourmet dinners and lectures on exotic destinations, maybe trade shows where door prizes are drawn, or maybe even a FAM (familiarization) trip where you go on a vacation as the guest of the supplier either for free or at a greatly reduced rate.

I love to travel. I've been around the world 3 times. I flew to Australia for free. I flew to Egypt for free. I stayed in a hotel in the Virgin Islands for a week for free. I flew to Paris for 19.00. I flew to Acapulco for $75.00. Everything was above board, because I am a travel agent. We usually get 75% to 90% off of Y class airline fares. We stay at hotels for a fraction of the rack rate. I've always wanted to travel like a millionaire, but never had a million dollars. I weigh too much to be a flight attendant, and I hate wearing pretentious suits. But as a travel agent I can wear anything I want and work when I want, because my office is a small desk and computer in the corner of my basement. I am an "Independent Agent" as it is known in the travel world, and I'm cashing in on this multi billion dollar industry. So many of my friends have asked me how they can become a travel agent. It's easy work and lots of fun, but you probably didn't know that, because the industry keeps this gold mine to themselves. Think about it, if everyone becomes a travel agent then who will be the clients? Like the old saying goes, it's not what you know, it's who you know. If you know people who will come to you when they want to travel, then you can arrange their travel and make a commission from the sales. Becoming a travel agent lets you enjoy the best life has to offer. You can receive cold hard cash, luxurious travel at incredible discounts, and the freedom to be your own boss and run your own life. My course teaches you how to become a travel agent from your own home. All you need is a telephone, email, and access to internet to begin. Becoming a travel agent is your passport to a world of excitement, and an opportunity that can change your life forever. Becoming a travel agent has been one of the smartest career moves I've taken; it has created a way to make my dreams come true. If exploring the world is in your dreams too, then this course is for you.

TRAVEL AGENTS
- Are Matchmakers
- Try out vacations
- Recommend Tours
- Receive Commission

Travel agents are matchmakers between tourists and suppliers. Travel agents don't actually sell anything. They are simply finding buyers for products that suppliers are selling. They work under a host travel agency who is licensed to receive commissions from the suppliers. The host agency splits part of the commission received from the supplier with the travel agent. A travel agent is neither a buyer, nor a seller, but rather is someone who knows how to find a great buyer and a great seller, and match them together. A good travel agent knows his customer's desires and also knows the products that suppliers offer to the tourists.

How is a vacation and leisure travel agent different from a full service agent?

A full service agent works a lot with writing airline tickets, using a GDS / CRS, being an expert on a large variety of travel products. A vacation and leisure travel agent only works with a small slice of the supplier market, namely cruises and tour operators. A full service agent usually works by the hour, has been to travel agent school for 2 years, has several years' experience, and works with a large number of suppliers. The vacation and leisure agent doesn't usually know how to write airline tickets, doesn't want to learn how to do so, doesn't want to go to school for 2 years to learn geography and ticketing, doesn't want to get involved in the paperwork of the travel industry, doesn't want to be tied down to a close to minimum wage job, and doesn't want to be the boss's gopher. Vacation and leisure agents can have the exact same travel agent ID cards that the full service agents get, but only do a fraction of the work. We work on straight commission, work when we want to, usually only book the high-commission products such as cruises or air/hotel packages, and sell in a limited market, like Orlando, Las Vegas, and other traditional vacation destinations. Vacation and leisure agents work with suppliers who do all the boring work for us, and the hard work like writing airline tickets. We usually use tour operators to write our airline tickets and make hotel reservations for our customer. We call cruise lines and let them write out airline tickets for us. We get travel industry rates from suppliers too, after we have earned our credentials.

Very important note! Don't try to trick suppliers into giving you agent rates!

It is illegal to ask a supplier to give you a "travel agent rate" for your personal vacations before you have earned your credentials (plastic ID card, etc) as a travel agent. Until you have your credentials, you are just an associate.

TRAVEL

What is a supplier?

Suppliers are the principal providers of tour products. A supplier could be an airline, but vacation & leisure travel agents usually don't purchase airfare straight from the airline because in order for the fare to be commissionable, the agent must do the booking using a GDS (Global Distribution System) or CRS (Computer Reservation System). It's hard to learn how to use a GDS / CRS. You have to pay licensing fees to have CRS access, and since airlines usually pay no commission that it's not economically feasible. When a customer needs airfare, the vacation & leisure travel agent will obtain air arrangements from a tour operator, who will write the tickets then mail the documents.

About Airfares

Airfares ticketed through a CRS are known as "published airfares." Tourists are usually looking for a great price, rather than convenience. Published airfares are usually not the best choice for vacation customers. While they are convenient, they are not cheap. The longer the tourist delays before purchasing a published fare, the higher the price becomes...buying a last minute published fare can add a thousand or more dollars to the price of the ticket. Most published fares require a Saturday night stay over to receive a discounted rate, plus some type of advanced purchase, e.g. 7 or 14 or 21 days' advanced purchase. An advance purchase excursion fare is known as an APEX fare. Even APEX fares are generally more expensive than "unpublished fares." There are different types of unpublished airfares: 1) Charter 2) Bulk 3) Consolidator 4) Internet only.

Charter Airfares typically are the best priced fares

Charter Airfares offer the greatest value for your customer's dollar. A charter flight is a type of flight which is booked exclusively for the use of a certain group of people. A tour operator rents the entire plane then disburses seats to its customers. Usually, charter flights are non-stop and go only to vacation destinations. Charters are common to Las Vegas, Florida, Mexico, and large international cities. Tour operators would not charter flights to places like Casper Wyoming, because there would not be enough demand for the flights. It is common for a charter flight to run only once a week, so if a customer misses the flight they are out of luck until the next flight returns. Most tour operators offer both charter air plus some sort of hotel package and ground transfers. Charter flights are not required to leave on time. They leave when they are ready to leave. If they need a part for the plane, the passengers wait until the mechanics are finished. Charters tend to have more seats in the aircraft than do scheduled flights. Always try to find out if a charter flight is available for your customer's vacation. The customer can save half price and more by going charter. Charter fares usually go down the closer it gets to the departure date so the tour operator can fill the flight. Buy 1 get 1 free are common promotions on charters. Charters typically go to smaller, less congested airports that the large airlines don't go to. For example, charters usually fly through Midway Airport rather than O'Hare, or London Gatwick rather than Heathrow, or Saint Petersburg rather than Tampa.

Bulk Airfares require they be combined with a second product

Bulk Airfares offer the next greatest value for your customer's dollar. A bulk fare is sold in conjunction with a second product like a hotel package, a cruise, or a car rental. Tour operators obtain large blocks of seats on scheduled airlines, then put them into a package which vacationers can purchase. Since the airlines do not want direct competition from the tour operator, they require that the airfare always be purchased only as one element in a vacation package. The great thing about bulk airfares is that the standard airfare rules do not apply because the ticket is not purchased directly from the airline, it's purchased from a tour operator. Bulk airfares usually don't require the Saturday night stays or advance purchase. When a passenger needs to fly somewhere at the last minute, it's usually cheaper to buy a bulk airfare and throw away the second item (like hotel stay) just to take advantage of the pre-negotiated rate on the bulk airfare. Usually, published airfares are non-refundable and non-changeable. If the tourist buys a bulk fare package, the tour operator sets the rules for refunds and exchanges. For a small fee, tourists can usually buy trip cancellation insurance when they book the trip. Sometimes that insurance lets the guest cancel the entire vacation without penalty, or for a very small fee. It's much better than buying an expensive published airfare which is non-refundable. Bulk fare tickets are issued for scheduled carriers, so your customer can be sitting on a Delta Airlines aircraft next to a person who paid the published fare. The important thing to remember is that bulk airfares are not sold directly by the airlines, they are sold by a second party.

Consolidator Tickets are sold primarily for international flights

Consolidator Tickets are sold by companies who contract with scheduled air carriers to offer airfares to the public at pre-negotiated rates. The consolidator usually agrees with the airlines to unload a large volume of seats to the public in exchange for being able to sell the seats at a set price. If the published fares go up, the consolidator still gets to sell at the pre-negotiated rate until his contract expires. In England, consolidators are called Bucket Shops. The London Times lists a huge number of consolidators who have airfares to points beyond London. Often, the cheapest fares to Africa would be to buy two tickets – one to England, then a second one from England to the final destination.

Internet Only airfares are sold on the internet only. They are not commissionable

Internet Only airfares are sold only on the internet. They are not commissionable. If you book one of the flights for a customer, you are doing so at a "net" rate. Net means that no commission is built into the airfare. If you book one of these fares for a customer, you will not get paid anything. Internet Only fares can be very cheap, especially for flights that are offered at the last minute when carriers are trying to dump empty seats on undersold routes. Each airline publishes their internet specials on their respective web sites. If a passenger only wants you to arrange his airfare, but not a hotel stay (and you can't get the passenger to his destination on a charter flight) then you probably should tell the customer to book his own flights on the internet. You are a vacation and leisure travel agent, not a full service agent.

About Hotels

Hotels, like airfares, can be purchased from a tour operator to save your customer money. Tour operators purchase hotel nights in huge blocks at bulk rates, so they are able to pass their buying clout on to you. Tour operators also have representatives who go to the hotels to inspect them, so you can feel safer buying from a tour operator rather than just picking a hotel blindly from a directory. Usually, tour operators throw in extra things like a coupon booklet or free admission to a museum or whatnot with the hotel package. If a customer states they want to stay at a particular hotel, just call that hotel and ask them for the names of tour operators which offer their hotel in a package. If they tell you no one sells their hotel in a package, this is a red flag!

Either the hotel has something dreadfully wrong with it, or you are talking to an uninformed employee at the hotel. In case of the latter, ask to speak with the reservations manager at the property.

About Cruises

Cruises offer the best vacation value for the dollar. Ships sail on all the waters of the Earth, to more than 1,800 ports of call from Alaska to Zanzibar. Included in the cruise price are meals, entertainment, activities, accommodations, and service. Your "floating palace" will take you to exotic islands without the struggle of connecting flights or having to check in and unpack at each location. The staff speak English, even if you are in an exotic port like Bora Bora. You can have as many meals as you like, and it can be American food if you're not into tribal / exotic foods. At dinner you can order more than one entrée, you can have meals taken to your stateroom (cabin), you can shop and gamble on board, even taken in movies. The water on a cruise is safe to drink, you don't have to worry about exotic spiders crawling on the floor all time while in a tropical country, and your kids can't go far if they get separated from you (whether intentional or not). Cruise ships have baby sitters, kids' programs, and shows. Cruises offer the ability to get up close to nature, and can take you places comfortably to remote islands where perhaps there are no hotels, running water, or electricity. You can meet interesting people on cruises, or just stay in the room and enjoy room service. In the event of an impending storm, the ship can divert its course to keep passengers safe.

Caribbean Cruise Itineraries

There are 3 basic Caribbean Cruise itineraries: East, West, and South. The Eastern cruises are for people who love to shop. Those guests would typically visit St. Thomas, St. Croix, and San Juan, where a zillion shops line the streets offering gold, linens, porcelain, fashions, etc.. These typically leave from Ft. Lauderdale. Western cruises typically leave from Florida and go to Cozumel, Playa del Carmen, Cayman Islands, and Jamaica, and they are for people who love sun and sand. Athletic, young adults typically like the western cruises, where they can enjoy parasailing, scuba, and lots of beach activities. The southern cruises go to the exotic islands like Martinique, Curaçao, Barbados, St. Martin, Grenada, etc. Travelers who really love experiencing a foreign culture would like the southern itineraries.

Booking travel products

Remember, the supplier does all the work.
Your job is to find the customer.

Booking travel is so easy! All you have to do make sure the supplier has all the information they want to know about the guest, and that the guest has all the information they want to know about the supplier. You are the independent agent who is making a reservation in the name of the agency, for example, Anton Anderssen Travel. You are an agent, not an agency. An agency is licensed, but you, an independent associate of Anton Anderssen Travel, are not licensed. Only agencies can be licensed, not individuals. You make reservations for your friends and family using the license numbers and contracts of your host agency, Anton Anderssen Travel. After the guest returns from his trip, the supplier will mail a commission check to Anton Anderssen Travel, which is shared with you.

You should limit the number of suppliers you use. It's better to know a few good suppliers really well than to try to guess about the reliability of a zillion different ones. After a while, you begin to learn which tour operators offer good service and good prices. Listed in this book are suppliers that agents often use for booking travel.

First determine where your customer wants to go then match him with a supplier offering that vacation

The first step is to find out where the customer wants to go. If he wants to go to Las Vegas, you will probably call America West Vacations. If he wants to go to Florida, you will probably call Delta Airlines Vacations. If he wants to go to Hawaii, you will probably call Blue Sky Tours Hawaii. There are other suppliers who will go to various destinations, and their destinations will change from time to time. The value packed tour operators will usually only offer seasonal departures. Funjet may offer vacation packages to the Bahamas in the winter, but not in the summer. You have to determine which suppliers are going where, and when. You do this by consulting their websites. You can also visit the websites to request brochures to hand out to your customers. You need to write your phone number on the back of the brochures so the customer calls you to make his booking, not the tour operator directly. That will cut you out of the sale. If your customer already has a vacation option put on hold with a supplier, you can call the supplier and tell them that Anton Anderssen Travel is taking over the booking, and you give the supplier our account information.

Call suppliers to get price quotes — **The next step** is to get price quotes for your customer. The supplier can usually put vacation options on hold for a week while the customer decides whether to buy the vacation. The supplier may need a deposit. The deposit is either refundable or non-refundable. You have to ask. You should always ask the supplier if they offer insurance in case the customer has to back out or can't make the trip for whatever reason. If so, add it to the price of the package, and let the customer know this is one of the features of the trip. If the customer refuses to buy insurance, make sure he gives you a signed statement saying he releases you and Anton Anderssen Travel from responsibility for not choosing travel interruption insurance.

Setting up the reservation
When you set up a reservation with a tour supplier, it's a good idea to have the customer on the line at the same time so each can answer one another's questions. This eliminates a lot of misunderstandings and telephone tag. After you have connected on the phone with your customer, press the flash button, and you will get a stutter dial tone. Now you can dial the supplier. Tell the supplier you are calling from Anton Anderssen Travel, and have a customer on the phone. Give our account information to the supplier. After the supplier is ready for your customer's information, press the flash button again, and it will bring all 3 of you into 1 conversation. The supplier can ask your customer for the destination information, ages of guests, seating preferences, dates of travel, etc. Let the supplier do most of the work for you. Take notes, writing down what the customer says. Record the credit card numbers, etc.

Luggage When speaking about luggage restrictions, be careful to specifically use the word luggage, e.g. "How much luggage may the customer take on this trip?" You may want to eliminate the word "baggage" from your conversation when speaking to suppliers from other countries, where the English word "baggage" will refer to 1) A woman of loose morals; a prostitute or 2) A romping, saucy girl (see dictionary.com entry for baggage). Also note that baggage refers to the entire collection of trunks, bags, parcels, and suitcases / valises - the whole variety of storage devices, mail bags, guitars, golf clubs, wheelchairs, and anything else that an airline transports in its cargo compartment. Therefore, a lady will be checking her luggage or her valise, not her "baggage."

Credit Cards

If the customer is paying the deposit, or any other amount by credit card, the supplier is the one who gets the approval. Make sure you write down the approval number. If the customer would like to apply for a charge card from the supplier, or some sort of finance plan from the supplier, now is the time to make the request. Your customer can finance his next Carnival cruise vacation with the simple 24-month Fun Finance Plan Call 1-800-728-1305 to apply. After the customer makes a purchase with his charge card, ask him to write you a note with his signature stating he gives permission to Anton Anderssen Travel and the supplier (for example, Carnival) to use your customer's charge card as payment for the trip. Otherwise, the customer could try to dispute the payment, and you would legally become responsible for paying for your customer's trip. Get the permission in writing to use a customer's charge card. It is very important. Make sure you have the supplier charge the customer's entire amount to the charge card, not the customer's price minus commission. You are not allowed to give Anton Anderssen Travel's commission away to the customer as a gift. If you fail to pay the supplier the whole amount owed by the customer, you are committing fraud. If your customer has no credit card, it would be a good idea for you to have a company credit card which you can use to call in the payments to the supplier. You can get a free business checking account at TCF Bank, and they will give you a free debit card to use which pulls funds from the account. The customer hands you money, you put the money in the bank, then you tell the supplier your debit card number. Remember you must always give the supplier the customer's entire vacation price (gross), not the net (gross minus commission). The first time you violate this requirement, it will be grounds for terminating your relationship with the travel agency. Similarly, sending in a check to a supplier that cuts out the agency commission is fraud, and will be considered employee theft.

When the customer checks in at the airline, they can do a fast check-in by sliding their credit card into the kiosk. It will bring up their reservation, allow them to choose seats, issue them a boarding pass, and let them declare luggage amounts. This will save them lots of time.

U.S. Bank and Northwest Airlines have a VISA Check Card that offers air miles for purchases. The NW WorldPerks VISA Check Card offers one Northwest Airlines mile for every $2 spent. However, the U.S. Bank/NWA debit card carries a $20 annual fee. Visit http://www.usbank.com/ or call 1-800-890-BANK ext. 9101 to apply by phone. Using this check card could accrue miles very quickly for free tickets to Hawaii and Europe for yourself!

Please be aware of your customer's travel rights. See http://www.mytravelrights.com/

Collateral is another word for sales promotion material. It can be brochures, videos, posters, and so forth. The convention and visitors' bureaus of cities typically provide these items. Also, tour operators will have brochures with info about the products they offer.

Here are some fax numbers to request free travel promotion collateral:

Kauai Hawaii 808 246 9235

Hawaii Big Island 808 961 2126

Maui 808 244 1337

Hawaii State 800 847 4844

Tax Advantages

When you become an independent contractor, you receive certain tax advantages. There are considerations to keep in mind when it comes to writing off your independent travel agency expenses. Be sure that you filled out a "Conducting Business under an assumed name" / DBA form and filed it with your county clerk before you start taking business expense write-offs.

For-Profit versus Hobby: How to use IRS guidelines to make your home-based travel business a "for profit" enterprise and avoid the dreaded hobby-loss limitations.

Overview Should your home-based travel activity incur a tax loss in any tax year, you want the activity classed as a business so that you can deduct your losses. Tax law gives no loss deductions for activities not carried on to make a profit. Activities you do as a hobby, or mainly for sport or recreation, come under this limit.

Application The limit on not-for-profit losses applies to individuals, partnerships, estates, trusts, and S corporations. It does not apply to corporations other than S corporations.

Expectation of Profit Although the IRS does not require a "reasonable expectation of profit," your facts and circumstances must show that you entered the home-based travel activity, or continued the activity, with the objective of making a profit. The IRS grants a profit motive if you prove that you have a small chance of making a large profit.

Intent Whether your business meets the test to be a business is a question of fact that depends on an analysis of your intent as determined from all facts and circumstances.

Desire Income To be a business, you must be involved in your home-based travel business with continuity and regularity and your primary purpose for the activity must be for income or profit. A sporadic activity, a hobby, or an amusement diversion does not qualify as a business.

Presumption of Profit The IRS presumes you carry on your home-based travel activity for profit if it produces a profit in at least three of the last five tax years, including the current year. You can rely on this presumption every time, unless the IRS shows it is not valid.

Proving Profit Intent When You Have Losses If you fail the three-out-of-five test, you may still deduct losses if you can prove that your home-based travel activity operated as a business. The IRS lists nine factors that may be important in establishing a profit motive:

Businesslike Manner The fact that you carry on your home-based travel activity in a businesslike manner and maintain complete and accurate books and records may indicate that the activity is engaged in for profit.

Expertise You help your profit motive when you study accepted business practices for your home-based travel activity and consult with those who are expert therein. You especially help your cause when you carry on your travel activity as directed by the experts. Failure to follow expert advice suggests lack of profit intent, unless you can show that your new or superior techniques may produce profits.

Time and Effort The fact that the taxpayer devotes much of his personal time and effort to carrying on an activity, particularly if the activity does not have substantial personal or recreational aspects, may indicate an intention to derive a profit. If you depend on income from your travel business for your livelihood, you show strong intent to make a profit.

Asset Appreciation The IRS accepts profit from appreciation as part of your profit motive.

Prior Success The fact that the taxpayer has engaged in similar activities in the past and converted them from unprofitable to profitable enterprises may show that he is engaged in the present activity for profit, even though the activity is presently unprofitable.

Income and Loss History A series of losses during start-up does not mean the activity is not engaged in for profit. However, where losses continue beyond the period ordinarily required to make the travel operation profitable, that excess period may suggest that the activity is not being engaged in for profit. A series of years where your travel activity produces net income would, of course, be strong evidence that the activity is engaged in for profit.

Occasional Profits An occasional small profit compared to large losses does not show that you engaged in the travel business to make a profit. However, substantial profit, though only occasional, suggests that an activity is engaged in for profit. Moreover, an opportunity to earn a substantial ultimate profit in a highly speculative venture indicates that the activity is engaged in for profit even though you generate only losses.

Your Other Income If you attempt to make a living from your home-based travel business, you usually establish a profit motive and can deduct your losses. Substantial income from sources other than your travel business may indicate that your travel activity is not engaged in for profit especially if there are personal or recreational elements involved.

Personal Pleasure or Recreation Your personal motives for the travel activity may suggest that the activity is not engaged in for profit, especially when you have recreational or personal elements involved. On the other hand, an activity that lacks any appeal other than profit suggests a profit motive. However, your intent to derive profit "does not" have to be your exclusive or sole intent. An activity will not be treated as not engaged in for profit merely because the taxpayer has purposes or motivations other than solely to make a profit. Also, the fact that the taxpayer derives personal pleasure from engaging in the activity is not sufficient to cause the activity to be classified as not engaged in for profit if the activity is in fact engaged in for profit as evidenced by other factors whether or not listed above.

Hobby-loss Limits If tax law classes your travel activity as a hobby, it limits your deductions to:

No more than your income from the hobby.

Reduced by 2% of adjusted gross income - because you report your hobby on Schedule A. Moreover, you may not carry over any unused losses from the current year to any future year.

Planning Tip Make your travel activity a business, have fun, and enjoy your profits. That way, should you experience a few loss years, you secure your loss deductions.

Filing Tip Do not agree to make a profit in three of the first five years by filing IRS Form 5213. Instead, make your travel activity a business, keep good records, and attempt to make a profit. Unlike a hobby, if you fail to make a profit in your business, you may deduct your losses.

Fam Trip Tax Deductions Learn the secrets to writing off 100% of travel agent familiarization trips and using travel rules to sell more travel to your business clients.

Definitions Tax law allows you to deduct travel expenses incurred while away from home in pursuit of business. If your trip required you to sleep or rest away from your principal place of business, you were away from home and in travel status.

Pursuit of Business You pursue your business when you pursue your current livelihood. This requires much more effort than entering an activity to make a profit. You travel in pursuit of your business when your travel is: 1) Appropriate and helpful to the development and maintenance of your business. 2) With the intent to secure a business benefit. 3) Customary and usual within your business community. When you travel in pursuit of your existing business needs, your travel is deductible immediately as a business expense. The law allows the deduction for "carrying on" the business and thus presumes that the business already exists.

Two Categories of Expenses Your travel expenses fall into one of two categories: 1) Transportation to business-destination expense 2) Business-day expenses. In addition to travel expenses, you may also incur expenses directly connected to your business activity, such as "familiarization" expenses.

Familiarization Travel for Travel Agents

Example 1 Deduct 100% of trip to Hawaiian Islands. Anita Flores, a travel agent, plans to market family and group travel to Hawaii. She and Robert, her employee/husband, take a 7-day trip to Hawaii. Each day, they familiarize themselves with and critique local hotels, restaurants, theaters, amusement activities and recreational activities.

Example 2 Deduct 100% of trip to Scotland and Ireland. Jack Smith, a travel agent and avid golfer, plans to market golf tours to Scotland and Ireland. He and Jill, his employee/wife, take a 15-day trip to Scotland and Ireland. Each day they visit, critique and survey gold courses and familiarize themselves with local tourist activities.

Example 3 Deduct 100% of trip to Orlando, Florida Pat Jones, a travel agent, plans to market family and group travel to Orlando. She and Fred, her employee/husband, take a 7-day trip to Orlando accompanied by their children, ages 10 and 12, who also work in the business. Each day they visit tourist attractions and the family provides Pat with daily critiques and reviews of their activities.

Example 4 Deduct 100% of cruise ship travel Tony Alvarez, a travel agent, plans to market cruise ship vacations to families and groups. Every three or four months, he and Melba, his employee/wife, take a 3 or 4-day cruise to familiarize themselves with different cruise lines and destinations.

Example 5 Deduct 100% of FAM trips sponsored by resorts and cruise lines Even on "no cost" or "free" familiarization trips, you will still be out-of-pocket on some types of expenses. The additional expenses are deductible as business write-offs when directly connected to your business activity.

Caution: Be advised that the burden of proof for such deductions would be greater than normal. You must be able to clearly demonstrate that time and effort is expended to profit from your travel activities. Keep detailed records of your travel activities and promotional activities including written critiques, personal recommendations, photographs and video tapes, brochures and marketing materials, direct mail promotions, speeches to civic and social clubs, etc.

Transportation Rules (based on trip days)

Rule: You deduct business transportation expenses to the extent that your trip passes a test for deducting transportation.

Primary-purpose Test: The primary purpose test applies to the costs of transporting yourself to and from a business destination within the 50 United States and District of Columbia. Under this test, if you spend more days on business than you spend on pleasure, you deduct 100% of your transportation. If your trip is not primarily business, you may deduct nothing for transportation.

General Foreign Travel Test: If more than 75% of your days are business days, you may deduct 100% of the costs of transporting yourself to a foreign destination. A foreign destination is outside the 50 United States and District of Columbia. If you spend 75% or less of your days on business, you may deduct transportation expenses based on the ratio of business days to total trip days.

One-week Foreign Travel Test: You may deduct 100% of the transportation to a foreign destination when your trip involved one business day and is less than seven days, excluding the day of departure.

Foreign Rules Are Clear. Tax law contains clear examples of business days for foreign travel. Although the definitions for foreign deductions are generally stricter than those for domestic travel, they provide a definition guideline that is high useful. Following are the stricter foreign-travel rule definitions of business days.

Work Days: You count as a business day any day during which your principal activity during normal business hours is the pursuit of business. In other words, you must work four (4) hours and one (1) minute (more than half the day).

Tried-to-Work Days. You count as a business day any day that circumstances beyond your control prevented you from actively pursuing your business objectives.

Weekends, Holidays, and Standby Days: Weekends, holidays, and other necessary standby days count as business days when sandwiched by business days during a trip you conduct with reasonable dispatch. The weekend rule applies only where it would not be practical to return home from your business destination for the weekend because of time required or expense involved.

Saturday Night Travel: Airlines generally charge you less if you stay at your destination over a Saturday night. If you save money by staying over Saturday night, you count the stay over days as business days.

Travel Days: Travel days are business days. To ensure business-day status, your total portal-to-portal-in-transit and business-activity time for the day should exceed four hours.

Methods of Transportation

Rule: You may transport yourself to and from a business destination by: Automobile, Airplane, Train, Boat. It makes no difference if your car is large or small, if you fly coach or first class, or if it is a private plane. Transportation costs are deductible in full, except luxury boats.

Luxury Boat Deduction Limits: Your water transportation deduction may not exceed twice the highest per diem rate allowed the executive branch of government for travel in the contiguous United States.

Example: On July 7, 1999, when the per diem rate was $180.22, you took a six-day trip from New York to London on QE2. You may deduct no more than $2,160 ($180 x 2 x 6 days).

Car Strategy: Transport family 300 miles toward business destination. Consider driving your car on a combined business and pleasure trip! When you drive 300 miles in direct route toward the destination, the day counts as a business day, just as it does for an IRS agent. Therefore, you:

1) Count the day as a business day to satisfy the 51/49 test; and 2) Deduct your costs of sustaining life while on the road for that day.

Meals and lodging expenses of family members other than the taxpayer do not qualify for deduction. If the cost of lodging is $80 for single occupancy and $95 for family, you deduct only $80.

Example: You put the family in the car and spend four days driving to and from Chicago and Washington, D.C., for a three-day convention. You then spend six days sightseeing. Your trip is primarily business because you spent 7 of 13 days on business. You deduct: 1) 100% of the transportation 2) 7 days of sustaining business life on-the-road costs.

Travel for Your Hobby

Should you travel for your hobby, your expenses, including travel, may not exceed your income from the hobby. Worse, you may not deduct any hobby losses - not in the current year or against income of a future year.

Example: You raise dairy cows for a hobby. Your gross income from sales is $1,000. You spend $500 in interest to finance the cows and $900 to feed them. Your $400 loss is not deductible this year, or in any future year.

Licenses in More Than One State: The IRS notes that some taxpayers have licenses to do business in more than one state. Such taxpayers may have legitimate reasons for business travel.

Get Education Out of Town: You may deduct the travel costs necessary to obtain education or attend a meeting or convention. Tax law does not require study in your back yard, even when the same courses are available there. The Senate noted that a French scholar may deduct his travel to study at the Sorbonne. Similar, a Texas professor deducted the cost of travel and living in Hawaii while studying for her Ph.D. in Hawaii.

Meet With Colleagues: You could travel to meet with colleagues in other parts of the country to learn new skills.

Job Hunting Trips: Rev. Rul. 77-16 holds that you may deduct transportation and travel to seek new employment in your current trade or business. Rev. Rul. 75-120 notes that you may deduct the search expenses whether the search is successful or unsuccessful. The IRS notes that time spent on the search compared to time spent on personal activities determines if the trip is primarily business or personal.

Deducting the Cost of Bringing Your Spouse to the Convention:

Tax law gives no deduction for travel of a spouse, dependent, or other individual accompanying the taxpayer on business travel unless: 1) The spouse, dependent, or other companion is an employee of the taxpayer. 2) The travel of the spouse, dependent, or other companion is for a bona fide business purpose. 3) Travel expenses of the spouse, dependent or other person would otherwise be deductible.

The law makes it clear that your spouse not only must be an employee, but also must travel for a bona fide business purpose. You get no travel deduction when you bring your spouse to: 1) Be the socially gracious spouse 2) Staff the hospitality suite 3) Be the assigned fraternizer 4) Type notes, eat lunches, and dinners. The presence of your children at the travel site helps negate the business aspects of your spouse's travel.

Video Tapes at Resorts You get no deduction for a business seminar that gives you a videotaped lecture that you may watch at your convenience. If you must watch the tape at the seminar or convention site, the video tape counts just as if you attended a live lecture.

Observation: You obviously invite more scrutiny if you attend a resort-based session that consists solely or primarily of video tape.

Convention Delegate You may deduct the costs of attending a convention as a delegate if you can show that attendance advanced your personal business interests.

Example: You attend the Toastmasters International convention as a delegate. You can prove that such attendance generated more revenue than you spent at the convention. You may deduct the costs.

Travel Cost of Looking for a Rental Property If your travel results in the acquisition of investment property, the travel is a start-up cost that you may amortize over 60 months beginning when you place the property in service as a rental. We assume here that you are not in the business of investing in real estate.

Attempt to Purchase If your travel fails to secure a specific property that you identified and attempted to purchase, you may deduct your travel costs as a business loss.

Special Rules for Conventions

U.S. Cruise Ship Conventions: You may deduct up to $2,000 for the cost of a cruise-ship convention or meeting provided: 1) The meeting relates directly to the active conduct of your business. 2) The ship is a registered U.S. vessel. 3) All ports of call are in the United States or its possessions. 4) You attach written statements, signed by you and the program sponsor, to your tax return.

North American Conventions: You may not deduct a foreign convention unless it is as reasonable for the convention to be outside the United States as to be within the United States. Reasonable is the basic rule. Of course, the law contains exceptions! Convention trips to defined North American destinations do not have to pass the foreign-trip reasonableness test. The defined North American area includes: American Samoa, Baker Island, Barbados, Bermuda, Canada, Costa Rica, Dominica, Dominican Republic, Grenada, Guam, Guyana,. Honduras, Howland Island, Jamaica, Jarvis Island, Johnston Island, Kingman Reef, Marshall Islands, Mexico, Micronesia, Midway Islands, Northern Mariana Islands, Palau, Palmyra, Puerto Rico, Saint Lucia, Trinidad and Tobago, U.S. Virgin Islands, USA, Wake Island.

To deduct a convention trip to the above destinations, you must make the trip during the ordinary and necessary course of your business. In other words, you must make the trip for business purposes. For example, you must have a business reason to attend the convention.

Foreign Conventions Tax law states: "In the case of any individual who attends a convention, seminar, or similar meeting which is held outside the North American area, no deduction shall be allowed under Section 162 for expenses allocable to such meeting unless the taxpayer establishes that the meeting is directly related to the active conduct of his trade or business and that, after taking into account in the manner provided by regulations prescribed by the secretary: 1) the purpose of such meeting and the activities taking place at such meeting, 2) the purposes and activities of the sponsoring organization or groups, 3) the residences of the active members of the sponsoring organization and the places at which other meetings of the sponsoring organization or groups have been held or will be held, and 4) such other relevant facts as the taxpayer may present, it is as reasonable for the meeting to be held outside the North American area as within the North American area."

Technical Note: The Senate Committee Report from which the foreign convention rules originate states: "The bill makes clear that the foreign convention provisions do not apply to normal business meetings for employees of a company."

Examples of U.S. Trips

Example 1: You travel from Seattle to Miami Thursday, work Friday, standby Saturday and Sunday, work Monday, and return home Tuesday. The six days qualify as business days. You deduct 100% of your transportation to and from Miami. You also deduct your costs of sustaining life for each of the six business days.

Example 2: Same as Example 1, except you vacation for four days at the end of your stay. Again, you deduct 100% of your transportation. You also deduct the same costs for the six business days. You do not deduct any costs for the four vacation days.

Example 3: You travel from Miami to Seattle Wednesday, work Thursday, layover Friday and Saturday to save travel costs with a lower airfare, and return home Saturday. You deduct 100% of your transportation. You also deduct your costs of sustaining life for each of the 5 days.

Example 4: You travel from San Diego to Philadelphia and spend 3 days working and 15 days playing. You deduct your costs of sustaining life for the three work days and nothing (zero, zip) for transportation.

Audit-Proofing Travel Deductions

Timely Records Required. Tax law effectively required you to record travel expenditures "at or near the time" you incurred the expenses. Timely records have a "high degree of credibility not present with respect to a statement prepared subsequent thereto when generally there is a lack of accurate recall."

Diary Entries Needed. Generally, when taxpayers lose court cases involving travel, the lack documentation, mainly entries in a diary.

What to Write Down

You must prove for each travel expenditure: 1) Amount: Amount of each separate expenditure for traveling away from home, such as cost of transportation or lodging, except that daily cost of a traveler's own breakfast, lunch, dinner, and incidentals may be aggregated, if set forth in reasonable categories, such as meals, gas and oil, and taxi; 2) Time: Dates of departure and return for each trip away from home, and number of days away from home spent on business; 3) Place: Destination or locality of travel, described by name of city or town or other similar designation; and 4) Business purpose: Business reason for travel or nature of the business benefit derived or expected.

Receipts Required Tax law required documentary evidence, such as receipts, paid bills, or similar evidence sufficient to support expenditures for: 1) Lodging, Any expenditure of $75 or more. Hint: Keep receipts for all expenses and record the places where you eat the meals, e.g., hotel, Burger King, etc.

Categories of Travel The IRS lists the following recognized categories of travel expenses: 1) Meals and lodging, both in route and at the final work destination; 2) Transportation costs, including air, rail or bus fares, and the costs of transporting baggage, sample case or display materials; 3) The allocable portion of operating and maintenance expenses of automobiles, house trailers, and airplanes; 4) Cleaning and laundry; 5) Telephone; 6) Public stenographer costs; 7) Costs of transportation between an airport or station and hotel, from customer to customer, and from one place of business to another, and 8) Tips incidental to the above expenses.

Cleaning and Laundry To deduct the cost of cleaning your clothes, you must get the clothes dirty while in travel status (out of town overnight).

Las Vegas

A very important vacation and leisure destination

Las Vegas! It's a 24 hour town that caters to guests of all ages. Casino gaming, top entertainment, performances, thrill rides, and great buffets are just a few reasons to visit Las Vegas. You will want to buy an air/hotel package from a tour operator such as FunJet for your guest. Your customer gets the best value when buying vacation items as part of a package. Remember to book directly at www.AntonFunJet.com and you don't need passwords.

LAS VEGAS STRIP HOTELS AND CASINOS

Algiers Hotel 1-800-732-3361
Bally's Hotel 1-800-634-3434
Barbary Coast 1-888-227-2279
Bellagio Hotel 1-888-987-6667
Bourbon Street 1-800-634-6956
Caesar's Palace 1-800-634-6661
Casino Royale 1-800-854-7666
Circus Circus 1-877-224-7287
Excalibur 1-800 937 7777
Flamingo Hilton 1-800-732-2111
Frontier 1-800-634-6966
Hardrock Hotel 1-800-473-7625
Harrah's 1-800-634-6765
Imperial Palace 1-800-634-6441
Klondike 1-702-739-9351
Las Vegas Hilton 1-800-732-7117
Luxor 1-800-288-1000

Mandalay Bay 1-877-632-7000
Maxims 1-800-634-6987
MGM Grand 1-800-929-1111
Mirage 1-800 627-6667
Monte Carlo 1-800-311-8999
New York NY 1-888-696-9887
Paris 1-877-796-2096
Riviera 1-800-634-6753
Sahara 1-800-634-6411
San Remo 1-800-522-7366
Stardust 1-800-634-6757
Stratosphere 1-888-99-TOWER
Treasure Island 1-800-944-7444
Tropicana 1-800-634-4000
Vacation Village 1-800-658-5000
Venetian 1-877-857-1861
Westward Ho 1-800-634-6803

DOWNTOWN HOTELS AND CASINOS

Binion's Horseshoe 1-800-622-6468
California 1-800-634-6255
El Cortez 1-800-634-6703
Fitzgeralds 1-800-274-5825
Four Queens 1-800-634-6045
Fremont 1-800-634-6182
Gold Spike 1-800-634-6703

Golden Gate 1-800-426-1906
Golden Nugget 1-800-634-3403
Plaza 1-800-634-6575
Lady Luck 1-800-523-9582
Las Vegas Club 1-800-634-6532
Main Street Station 1-800-465-0711
The Western 1-800-634-6703

The best value for Las Vegas Vacations is usually on America West Vacations, Future Vacations, or Funjet. They will write your airline tickets, hotel vouchers, car, and attraction vouchers. They can give you much better prices than you could get on your own. Funjet offers charter flights, which you can book for your customers who have hotel comps already. If you book through the standard Funjet website (not referring to www.AntonFunJet.com) you are doing so as an individual, not as a travel agent, and therefore they will not pay any commission. If the customer does not want to go on a Charter, tour companies can give you airfare from their private inventory, but you are required to purchase another item to make it a package, for example, car for a few days, or hotel stays for a few nights.

Aladdin If you enjoy shopping you'll love the Desert Passage Shopping Center

All Casinos Most casinos have matches lying around that are free for the taking. Help yourself! Place them in a jar for a great souvenir of your trip!

All Casinos Drinks are FREE if you are playing at the tables or slots. However, most people will tip the waitress $1.

All Casinos Valet Parking- Not exactly free but almost. In most cases a $1 tip when they bring back your car is sufficient.

All Casinos Plastic Cups - These cups/buckets are used by all casinos to hold your slot machine winnings are free. Collect them all, they will be valuable some day.

All Casinos Almost every casino will provide FREE decks of cards. Ask a pit person while you're playing.

All Casinos Parking - Almost every Las Vegas casino offers FREE parking. In some cases, usually downtown, you may need to get your parking ticket validated in the casino.

Bally's Free ride on the monorail to MGM Grand runs from 9:00 a.m. to 1:00 a.m., seven days a week. Runs average about ten minute intervals. Located by the Bally's pool area and exits at the MGM Grand parking garage area.

Bally's Free pull slot machine can be played once daily. Located between the Jubilee showroom and the Sportsbook.

Bellagio Free Water Fountain Show. Fantastic! Sunday's through Fridays at 5:00 p.m. to midnight. On Saturday's from 2:00 to midnight. Shows are presented every half hour (on the hour & half hour).

Bellagio Free monorail to the Monte Carlo. It runs from 8:00 a.m. to 4:00 a.m. seven days a week.

Bellagio Free tour of the Botanical Conservatory is a breath of fresh air. Hundreds of fresh flowers and real trees. Dome glass ceiling, open 24 hours and is located just past the hotel registration desk. Follow the signs.

Boulder Station Guadalajara Mexican Restaurant will give you a free lunch or dinner entree on your birthday. Must be 21 and have a valid I.D. which must be shown to your server. Only good on the actual day of your birthday.

Caesars Palace FREE Atlantis Water Show in the Fourm Shops. (At the end of the street by the Schwarz Toy Store). First show at 10:00 a.m. and the last show at 11:00 p.m., daily on the hour.

Caesars Palace FREE Caesar and Brutus Show in the Fourm Shops. (at the end of the street where Planet Hollywood restaurant is located.) First show at 10:00 a.m. and the last show at 11:00 p.m., daily, on the hour.

Circus Circus FREE clown show at the Adventuredome Theme Park daily at noon, 1 p.m., 3 p.m. and 4 p.m. Additional shows on Fridays and Saturdays at 6 p.m., 7 p.m., 8 p.m. and 9 p.m.

Circus Circus Visit the carnival midway located on the main casino mezzanine. thrilling circus acts including clowns, aerialists and jugglers are featured in the center ring. Sunday thru Thursdays from 11:15 a.m. to 11:45 p.m. every 45 minutes. Fridays and Saturdays 11:15 a.m. to 11:45 p.m. every half hour. All shows are FREE!

Circus Circus FREE monorail between the Circus Circus main building and its North Tower. It runs from 6 a.m. to 1 a.m., seven days a week.

Excalibur Merlin subdues fire-breating dragon in hotel's moat. Best viewed from the driveway or from the drawbridge. The fire breathing beast lurking in Excalibur's castle moat can be seen in battle every hour on the hour from 6 p.m. to midnight nightly, depending on weather conditions.

Excalibur The court Jesters Stage features free, live variety acts daily beginning at 10:00 a.m. The talented cast of 28 performers features singers, magicians, jugglers and contortionists. Acts are approx. 10 minutes in length and are presented every 45 minutes.

Excalibur FREE Monorail between Excalibur/Luxor/Mandalay Bay runs 24 hours a day and picks up riders every 8 minutes.

Flamingo Hilton The Wild Habitat has 14 penquins, 10 flamingos, assorted exotic birds, two albino turtles and koi. Open 24 hours a day on the terrace in the back next to the swimming pool.

Flamingo Hilton Free bus tour to the Flamingo Hilton in Laughlin. Includes free buffet and funbook. Call: (702) 735-5755

Freemont Street Experience An exciting pedestrian promenade located in downtown Las Vegas. It includes a misting system, retail cart, kiosks and FREE mall entertainment. Plus, a one-of-a-kind light and sound show derived from over 2 million lights and 540,000 watts of concert quality sound. Shows every night on the hour every hour beginning at dusk with the last show at midnight. http://www.vegasexperience.com

Golden Nugget The world's largest golden nugget is on display next to the gift shop and across from the entrance to the California Pizza Kitchen Restaurant.

Hard Rock The concierge desk, which is located just across from the hotel room registration, has a free "Rock Tour" map showing where all the rock and roll items are on display in the Hotel and Casino.

Harrah's FREE outdoor party right on the Strip, on the south side of Harrah's, called "Carnival Court." Fridays and Saturdays from 11:30 a.m. to 2:00 a.m. and Sundays thru Thursdays from 11:30 a.m. to midnight weather permitting.

Jackie Gaughan's Plaza Hotel/Casino A FREE key chain, with your own picture on it, can be obtained from the "Slot Club" booth next to the keno lounge. They take your picture and 40 minutes later you can come back and they give you a key chain with your picture on it!

Luxor FREE Monorail between Excalibur/Luxor/Mandalay Bay runs 24 hours a day and picks up riders every 8 minutes.

Mandalay Bay FREE Monorail between Excalibur/Luxor/Mandalay Bay runs 24 hours a day and picks up riders every 8 minutes.

MGM Grand Free admission to the Lion Habitat. The three-story habitat is located near the Studio 54 entrance and showcases a variety of lions and cubs, including Goldie, Metro and Baby Lion, a direct descendant of MGM's Studios' famous marquee lion. The Lion Habitat, a truly magnificent state-of-the-art showcase, features four separate waterfalls, overhangs, a pond and Acacia trees. The habitat is enclosed with skylights and walls reaching heights of 35 feet to provide maximum viewing for guests. Guests are afforded the opportunity to be encircled by lions at any time via a see-through walk way tunnel that runs through the habitat, allowing lions to prowl above and below. Hours of the habitat are 11 a.m. to 11 p.m., seven days a week.

MGM Grand Entertainment Dome always has free shows on most of the day. The adult musical acts are very good and change often. The Entertainment Dome is located across from the Studio 54 and past the Lion Habitat.

Mirage White tiger habitat. Behind the California Pizza Kitchen and across from the Gift Shop. Open 24 hours, seven days.

Mirage Erupting volcano. Show lasts about 3 minutes and can be seen nightly after dark, every 15-20 minutes until midnight.

Mirage FREE monorail to Treasure Island. It runs from 8 a.m. to 4 a.m., seven days a week.

Monte Carlo FREE monorail to Bellagio. It runs from 8 a.m. to 4 a.m., seven days a week.

Most Casinos Bell Captain's desk in most casinos have copies of various Las Vegas magazines. Check them out for money saving coupons.

New York-New York Sign up for the Slot Exchange (Slot Club) club card and receive 10 FREE pulls on their $1,000 Jackpot Slot Machine and a FREE entry into their Daily Slot Tournament.

Rio Masquerade Village Parade performances at 4, 6, 8 and 10 p.m. Dark Tuesday and Wednesday. Try standing underneath the floats as the balcony is really crowded. It's also the best way to catch some beads.

Riviera FREE pull on a huge slot machine. Near the main door. Everyone wins at least a deck of cards.

Riviera Mannequins from the performance of "La Cage" in a glass window in front of the casino.

Sahara The slot club offers each member one FREE and very interesting coupon book.

Sam's Town The free Laser Show in the Mystic Falls Park is on at 2:00 p.m., 6:00 p.m., 8:00 p.m. and 10:00 p.m. seven days a week in the back courtyard.

Slots-A-Fun Free popcorn is available 24 hours a day on the counter at the snack bar. Just take one!

Stardust Slot Club - FREE gaming diary, to keep track of your wins and losses, is available on request.

Sunset Station The Slot Club counter usually has free copies of "Strictly Slots Magazine" around the beginning of each month.

The Orleans FREE beads are given out for the asking at any change booth, but not at the main cashiers cage.

The Orleans Slot Club. If you are a member of their slot club they will mail to your home a coupon for free 2,500 slot club points. This coupon can be redeemed any time after your birthday up to the next 3 months.

Treasure Island Watch the FREE pirate show at Treasure Island's Buccaneer Bay from the safety on the shore as the pirate schooner Hispaniola sinks the British Navy frigate HMS Britannia. Performances: 4:00 p.m., 5:30 p.m., 7:00 p.m., 8:30 p.m., 10:00 p.m. and 11:30 p.m., seven days a week.

Tropicana Magician Rick Thomas's tiger habitat located in front of the hotel. FREE to the public, the habitat offers guests and passers-by a rare opportunity to get close to a few of nature's most majestic creatures. The habitat is open Saturday through Thursday, 1 to 10 p.m.

Tropicana FREE show "The Birdman of Las Vegas," everyday except Thursdays, in the Tropics Lounge. Showtimes are 11 a.m., 12:30 p.m. and 2 p.m.

Tropicana Outside the main entrance try a pull on the big slot machine. It's free and you will win something worthwhile, most likely a FREE ticket to the afternoon Rick Thomas magic show.

Venetian Take a stroll through their Grand Canal Shoppes and see the opera singers in their gondolas in the canal.

Westward Ho FREE ice cream is given out between 2 p.m. and 4 p.m., seven days a week.

You can refer your customers to www.AntonFunJet.com and it automatically is commissionable. All you have to do is tell them to let you know they made a booking so you can collect their documents from Anton Anderssen Travel, and collect your commission too.

Las Vegas CVB www.vegasfreedom.com www.lvcva.com They will mail out brochures and info. The websites list commissionable travel in Las Vegas.

Activities in Las Vegas

Caesars Palace Omnimax theater located within Caesars Palace shows entertaining and educational films on a 6 story high screen. Call for current shows 702-731-7900 (Admission Fee)
Circus-Circus Five acre theme park features a roller coaster kiddie rides, water flume and an arcade. Entry is free with ride tickets or unlimited passes available.
Oceanspray's Cranberry World Visitors to Cranberry world will know everything about cranberries when the tour is finished. Many interesting demonstrations and a cranberry juice sampling bar are found on this FREE self guided tour. Open daily 9 a.m.-5 p.m.
Ethel M Chocolate Factory Free admission to this self guided tour of a real chocolate factory. Learn how the candy is made and finish your tour with free candy samples!
Guinness World of Records More than 5,000 sq. feet of weird and unusual exhibits are on display. Fun for the whole family 9 a.m.-6 p.m. daily (Admission Fee)
Imperial Palace Auto Collection A collection of over 800 cars is rotated monthly with 200 on display at any one time. Truly a car lovers paradise, the Imperial auto collection features Presidential cars and the Deusenburg room. Daily 9:30 a.m.-11:30 p.m.(Admission Fee) Free admission vouchers can be found in most of the visitors magazines.
Liberace Museum Located in the Tropicana Hotel/casino the Liberace museum contains many of his famous costumes, the gold diamond studded piano much more. Daily 10 a.m.-5 p.m. (Admission Fee)
Neon Museum Visit the outdoor display and see the neon signs of the past from Las Vegas. Plaques with information on the history of the signs take you through this self guided tour. Located just beyond the Freemont Street Experience, admission is FREE
New York-New York Manhattan Express Ride the roller coaster around the Hotel perimeter and dive and twist like a pilot in a barrel roll. (Admission Fee) 702-740-6969 for more info
Sahara Speedworld Take the 8 minute virtual reality ride in a 3/4 scale Indy Car and feel speed and acceleration just like the real thing. Also offers two 24 seat 3-d simulator theaters (Admission Fee) Located at Sahara Hotel/Casino
Secret Garden of Seigfried and Roy The secret garden, located at The Mirage, is a paradise with lions, tigers, leopards and Dolphins Audio presentations describe the animals and their habits. (Admission Fee) Daily 11 a.m.-7 p.m. Closed Wednesdays

Star Trek The Experience Located in the Las Vegas Hilton, this attraction takes visitors through time to the 24th century aboard the USS Enterprise. History of Star Trek on display complete with costumes and models. Daily 11 a.m.-11 p.m. (Admission Fee)
Stratosphere Tower At 1,149 ft. tall the tower is the highest freestanding observation deck in America. Ride the roller coaster or take the Big Shot ride at the top of the tower for the thrill of a lifetime. Excellent location to view the neon lights of the strip. Daily 10 a.m.-1 a.m. (Admission Fee)
Venetian Gondola Rides For the romantic at heart, the gondolas of Venice is a relaxing ride . The gondoliers are noted for their urge to sing a ballad for you and your sweetheart as you travel through the winding canals. (Admission Fee)
World of Coca-Cola Ride 100 feet to the top of the world's tallest bottle of Coke. History on Coke and memorabilia make this unique retail attraction a good time for the family. Daily 10 a.m.-10 p.m. (Admission Fee)

In Las Vegas, you will walk more than usual. If you have back or feet problems, you will want to check with the larger hotels or a local medical supply company about renting an ECV (electric convenience vehicle). It's a motorized chair with a shopping basket in the front. There is a city bus that goes up and down the strip all day long, and it easily will accommodate ECVs by extending a lift ramp to the curb.

All visitors to Las Vegas need sun block, even if you are dark skinned. Buy it before you go to get the best price. You also must drink a lot more water than you normally would at home.

Company:	Contact:
Bellagio Gallery of Fine Art	**Information** 3600 Las Vegas Boulevard South Las Vegas, NV 89109 Phone: 702-957-9777 Fax: 702-693-7871
Driving 101	**Heather Lutz** 6915 Speedway Blvd Las Vegas, NV 89115 Phone: 702-651-6300 Fax: 702-651-6310 hlutz@driving101.com
Gameworks	**Information** 3785 Las Vegas Boulevard #10

	#10 Las Vegas, NV 89109 Phone: 702-432-4263 Fax: 702-895-7599
Lake Mead Cruises	**Ginny Gottfredson** Post Office Box 62465 Boulder City, NV 89006 Phone: 702-293-6180 Fax: 702-293-0343 info@lakemeadcruises.com
Las Vegas Natural History Museum	**Information** 900 Las Vegas Boulevard North Las Vegas, NV 89101 Phone: 702-384-3466 Fax: 702-384-5343 info@lvnhm.org
Lied Discovery Children's Museum	**Information** 833 Las Vegas Boulevard North Las Vegas, NV 89101 Phone: 702-382-3445 Fax: 702-382-0592 mail@ldcm.org
Skydive Las Vegas	**Information** 1401 Airport Road #4 Boulder City, NV 89005 Phone: 702-759-3483 Fax: 702-293-5684 skydivelv@eathlink.net
Star Trek: The Experience	**Information** 3000 Paradise Road Las Vegas, NV 89109 Phone: 702-732-5111
Wet 'N Wild	**Information** 2601 Las Vegas Boulevard South Las Vegas, NV 89102 Phone: 702-871-7811 Fax: 702-871-8060
Wynn Collection, The	**Information** 3145 Las Vegas Boulevard South Las Vegas, NV 89109

Las Vegas, NV 89109
Phone: 702-733-4100

Culinary Excursions

Mary Granger
PO Box 70833
Las Vegas, NV 89170
Phone: 702-892-9287
Fax: 702-892-9287
marygranger@culinaryexcursions.com

Shop America

Kathy Perkins
3013 Windy Surf Court
Las Vegas, NV 89128
Phone: 702-228-3010
shopamerica@cox.net

American Golf Corp.

Tim Lafferty
1911 E. Desert Inn Rd.
Las Vegas, NV 89109
Phone: 888-442-4653 x 234
Fax: 702-796-0922
tlafferty@americangolf.com

Callaway Golf Center

John Boreta
6730 Las Vegas Blvd. South
Las Vegas, NV 89119
Phone: 702-896-4100
Fax: 702-896-9754
jboreta@callawaygolfcenter.com

Greens of Las Vegas

Bob Babilino
4813 Paradise Road
Las Vegas, NV 89109
Phone: 702-740-7472
Fax: 702-795-2656
bbabilino@greensworldwide.com

Las Vegas Premier Golf Vacations

Robert Wantland
1785 Clear River Falls Lane
Henderson, NV 89012
Phone: 702-270-6639
Fax: 702-270-9065
rw@lvpgolfvacations.com

Professional Golf Services

Brad Swanger
10624 S Eastern Ave. Ste A443
Henderson, NV 89052
Phone: 702-693-6776
Fax: 702-693-5965
pro@thecaddyshack.com

pro@thecaddyshack.com

Revere Golf Club

Amy Spittle
2600 Hampton Rd
Henderson, NV 89052
Phone: 702-259-4653
Fax: 702-617-5750
aspittle@troongolf.com

Siena Golf Club

Mick Toscano
10575 Siena Monte Ave
Las Vegas, NV 89138
Phone: 702-838-4196
Fax: 702-562-0883
mtoscano@sunriseco.com

Silverstone Golf Club

Jim Stanfill
8600 Cupp Drive
Las Vegas, NV 89131
Phone: 702-562-3770 x 104
Fax: 702-562-3771
jstanfill@mggi.com

Aladdin Resort & Casino

Patty Blevins
3667 Las Vegas Blvd South
Las Vegas, NV 89109
Phone: 702-785-5032
Fax: 702-785-5049
pblevins@aladdin.com

Alexis Park

Carroll White
375 E Harmon
Las Vegas, NV 89109
Phone: 702-796-3307
Fax: 702-796-0766
carrollw@alexispark.com

Ameri Suites Las Vegas

Nancy MacDonald
4520 Paradise Rd
Las Vegas, NV 89109
Phone: 702-369-3366
Fax: 702-369-1689
losmlg@primehospitality.com

Arizona Charlies Boulder

Clay Harris
4575 Boulder Highway
Las Vegas, NV 89121
Phone: 702-951-5840
Fax: 702-951-9201
charris@arizonacharlies.net

Bally's Paris Flamingo	**Dottie Haas** 3555 Las Vegas Blvd South Las Vegas, NV 89109 Phone: 702-733-3342 Fax: 702-697-2688 haasd@flamingolasvegas.com
Barbary Coast	**Felicia Brizuela** 3595 S Las Vegas Blvd Las Vegas, NV 89109 Phone: 702-737-7111 Fax: 702-894-9954 fbrizuela@coastcasinos.net
Bellagio	**Room Reservations** 3600 Las Vegas Blvd South Las Vegas, NV 89109 Phone: 702-693-7111 Fax: 702-693-8546
Best Western Mardi Gras Inn	**Marilyn Wagner** 3500 Paradise Rd Las Vegas, NV 89109 Phone: 702-731-2020 Fax: 702-731-4005 mwagner@mardigrasinn.com
Days Inn Town Hall	**Tom Zerr** 4155 Koval Ln. Las Vegas, NV 89109 Phone: 702-731-2111 Fax: 702-731-1113
El Cortez Hotel & Casino	**Sophia Rasile** 600 E Fremont Las Vegas, NV 89101 Phone: 702-474-3625 Fax: 702-747-3626 srasile@elcortezhotelcasino.com
Embassy Suites Convention Center	**Shawna Wright** 3600 Paradise Rd Las Vegas, NV 89109 Phone: 702-947-7170 Fax: 702-893-0708 lascc-ds@hildon.com
Embassy Suites - Las Vegas Airport	**Tracy Neller** 4315 Swenson St Las Vegas, NV 89119 Phone: 702-765-6752 Fax: 702-765-6899

	Fax: 702-765-6899 tneller@remingtonhotels.com
Excalibur Hotel	**Sandi Schroder** 3850 Las Vegas Blvd South Las Vegas, NV 89109 Phone: 800-444-3430 Fax: 702-597-7087 sschroder@mrgmail.com
Four Queens Casino Hotel	**Becky Snyder** 202 Fremont St Las Vegas, NV 89101 Phone: 702-387-5151 Fax: 702-387-5185 bsnyder@fourqueens.com
Frontier Hotel	**Jann Karzer** 3120 Las Vegas Blvd South Las Vegas, NV 89109 Phone: 702-794-8400 Fax: 702-794-8401 jkarzer@msn.com
Golden Nugget	**Ken Haas** 129 E Fremont St Las Vegas, NV 89101 Phone: 702-386-8220 Fax: 702-386-8248 khaas@goldennugget.com
Harrah's Las Vegas	**Annette Weishaar** 3475 Las Vegas Blvd. South Las Vegas, NV 89109 Phone: 702-777-7858 Fax: 702-777-7791 aweishaar@lasvegas.harrahs.com
Hotel San Remo	**Louise Faure** 115 E Tropicana Ave Las Vegas, NV 89109 Phone: 702-597-6008 Fax: 702-739-7783 lfaure@sanremolv.com
Imperial Palace	**Robert E Bline** 3535 Las Vegas Blvd. South Las Vegas, NV 89109 Phone: 702-794-3286 Fax: 702-794-3368 rebline@imperialpalace.com

Lady Luck

Marsha Williams
206 N 3rd Street
Las Vegas, NV 89101
Phone: 702-953-4467
Fax: 702-383-0782

Las Vegas Reservation Bureau

Bob Light
1820 E Desert Inn Rd 2nd Floor
Las Vegas, NV 89109
Phone: 702-794-4490
Fax: 702-794-0611
bob@nrbinc.com

Luxor Hotel & Casino

Room Reservations
3900 Las Vegas Blvd South
Las Vegas, NV 89119
Phone: 702-262-4444
Fax: 702-262-4452

Mirage

Kelly Kimble
3400 Las Vegas Blvd. South
Las Vegas, NV 89109
Phone: 702-791-7396
Fax: 702-692-8126
kkimble@mirage.com

Monte Carlo Resort & Casino

Mike Catalano
3770 Las Vegas Blvd South
Las Vegas, NV 89109
Phone: 702-730-7300

Nevada Palace Hotel & Casino

Robert Braner
5255 Boulder Highway
Las Vegas, NV 89122
Phone: 702-458-8810
Fax: 702-458-3361
hotelnvpal@aol.com

New York New York Hotel & Casino

Joe Ward
3790 Las Vegas Blvd South
Las Vegas, NV 89109
Phone: 702-740-6092
Fax: 702-740-6810
wardj@nyforme.com

Rio

Annette Weishaar
3700 W. Flamingo Rd.
Las Vegas, NV 89103
Phone: 702-777-7858
Fax: 702-777-7791

	Fax: 702-777-7791 aweishaar@lasvegas.harrahs.com
Riviera Hotel & Casino	**Cindy Lataille** 2901 Las Vegas Blvd. South Las Vegas, NV 89119 Phone: 702-794-9278 Fax: 702-794-9635 clataille@theriviera.com
St Tropez Hotel	**Angela Corvello** 455 E Harmon Las Vegas, NV 89109 Phone: 702-369-5400 Fax: 702-369-8901 angelac@tarsadia.com
Super 8 Koval	**Shirley Kessler** 4250 Koval Lane Las Vegas, NV 89109 Phone: 702-794-0888 Fax: 702-794-3504 shirleyk@super8vegas.com
Terrible's Casino	**Michelle Fazio** 4100 Paradise Road Las Vegas, NV 89109 Phone: 702-733-7000 Fax: 702-691-2423 mfazio@terriblescasino.com
The Royal Resort	**Jim Shields** 99 Convention Center Drive Las Vegas, NV 89109 Phone: 702-735-6117 Fax: 702-735-2546 jshields@royalhotelvegas.com
Treasure Island	**Ann Hoff** PO Box 7711 Las Vegas, NV 89177-0711 Phone: 702-894-7111 Fax: 702-894-7788 ahoff@treasureisland.com

Tripreservations.com

Brian Kaskie
6145 Spring Mountain Rd
Las Vegas, NV 89146
Phone: 702-946-5241
Fax: 702-946-5255
brian@tripres.com

Tropicana Resort & Casino

Room Reservations
3801 Las Vegas Blvd South
Las Vegas, NV 89109
Phone: 800-634-4000
Fax: 702-739-2492
hotelres@tropicanalv.com

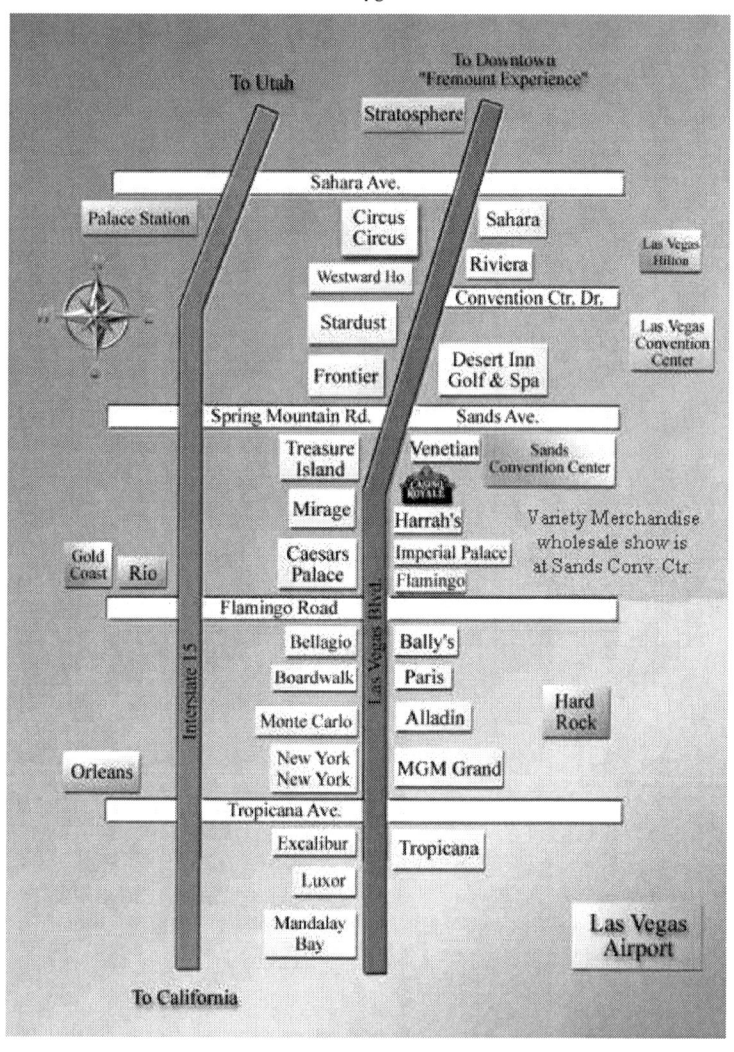

The "Strip" is officially called Las Vegas Blvd. There are also some cheaper hotels in the down town area. They surround a plaza which is covered by a steel canopy. The canopy has electric lights built into it which flash pictures and beautiful shapes, while music plays. This plaza is on Freemont Street. Near here is where the city bus depot is. You can catch a bus here to go down the strip. You can catch a free shuttle to Orleans at Barbary Coast.

Orlando

The most popular vacation destination in the world

Welcome to Orlando! This is the most popular vacation destination in the world. It is home to Disney World, Universal Studios Florida, Splendid China, Pirate's Dinner Adventure, Arabian Nights, and hundreds of attractions in Kissimmee and Lake Buena Vista. It is close to Port Canaveral and the Kennedy Space Center. It's also close to the attractions in Tampa and Daytona Beach.

For Universal Studios general information call 800 U ESCAPE For travel agent brochures / collateral for Universal Orlando call 800 550 1849 option #4. For your free Vacation Planning Kit and Orlando Magic Card call Orlando Orange County Visitor Center 888 291 5219 or 800-551-0181 Free Florida Vacation guides: call 888 6 FLA USA. Central FL Visitor's Bureau 800 828 7655. Orlando/Orange County Convention & Visitors Bureau Contact: (407) 363-5833; fax: (407) 370-5012; Web: www.orlandoinfo.com/trade. For free Disney World video call 800 241 1717

Isn't it a pain in the bum when you exit Orlando International Airport and instantly are soaked with two road tolls on the Beeline Expressway? The first one is one minute onto the road, and the second is just about a minute farther down the road. What nonsense! And the tolls are inflated, to top it off. The locals, who watch the tourists pay, laugh and manage to avoid these tolls by using the service drive for free. Take the north airport exit, which is also called 436, or Semoran Boulevard, toward downtown Orlando. As soon as you get out of the airport property there is a light at Frontage Road, also known as T.G. Lee Road. Turning left, you see a TGIFriday restaurant. Frontage Road is twisty and ends in a T. Turn left onto Tradeport Drive, known as Conway Road if you turn right. At the light, turn right onto McCoy Road. You'll see a 7-Eleven here. This is the Beeline tollway service road. Continue west on this road, going over Orange Avenue until you pass Florida Mall. Turn south (left) on Orange Blossom Trail, also known as 441. Go underneath Florida's Turnpike. Turn west onto the Beeline toward Disney World and Sea World. There are no further tolls at this point.

Disney Resort Listing

Value Resorts: All-Star Movies Resort, All-Star Music Resort, All-Star Sports Resort, Pop Century
Moderate Resorts: Caribbean Resort, Coronado Springs Resort, Port Orleans- Riverside Resort, Port Orleans- French Quarter Resort
Luxury Resorts: Animal Kingdom Lodge, Contemporary Resort, Grand Floridian Resort, Polynesian Resort, Yacht & Beach Club
Home Away From Home: Boardwalk Inn, Disney Institute, Fort Wilderness & Campground, Old Key West Resort, Wilderness Lodge
Other Disney Resorts: Dolphin Resort, Swan Resort
Downtown Disney Resort Area: Best Western Lake Buena Vista, Courtyard by Marriott, DoubleTree Guest Suites, Grosvenor Resort, Hilton Resort, Hotel Royal Plaza, Wyndham Palace Resort & Spa

Disney Theme Parks

Magic Kingdom: The original theme park. Cinderella's castle, Space Mountain, Haunted Mansion.
Epcot: Future World and Showcase of Nations. Giant Sphere, visit foreign countries.
Animal Kingdom: A safari adventure. Real exotic animals. Jungle Book characters.
MGM Studios: A Hollywood experience. This is a tribute to the stars.

Remember to buy your Disney park tickets from Disney Travel Company to get commissions. See appendix.

Spirit airlines usually has the lowest airfares Orlando.

Orlando Travel Agent Discounts
ATTRACTIONS

Busch Gardens
3605 E. Bougainvillea Ave.
Tampa, FL 33612
Tel: (813) 987-5404 or toll free 1-888-800-5447
Hours: 9:30 am - 6:30 pm with extended hours for summer and holidays
Description: A family amusement experience, which includes scenic zoological habitats, exciting rides, and thrilling live entertainment.
Discount: Agent and one guest receive 50% off. Each additional guest will receive $3.50 off. Must present IATA card & photo ID or embossed business card & ID. Accepted year round.

Daytona International Speedway Daytona USA
1801 W. International Speedway Blvd.
Daytona Beach, FL 32114
Tel: (904) 947-6404
Fax: (904) 947-6802
Hours: Monday through Sunday 9 am - 7 PM extended hours during special events.
Description: Daytona USA features exciting exhibits and interactive technology. Guided Speedway Tours available.
Discount: Agents receive free admission for Daytona USA and Speedway Tour. Present business card at Daytona USA's Guest Service's desk in the lobby of the attraction.

Fantasy of Flight
1400 Broadway Blvd. SE
Polk City, FL 33868
Tel: (863) 984-3500
Fax: (863) 984-9506
Hours: 9 am - 5 PM daily
Description: Florida's premier aviation attraction featuring realistic flight simulators, restoration shop tours, vintage aircraft displays and much more. Located between Orlando and Tampa, exit 21 on I-4.
Discount: Agents receive 50% off admission for 2 adults and 2 children. Must present IATA card for discount.

Florida Splendid China
3000 Splendid China Blvd.
Kissimmee, FL 34747
Tel: (407) 396-7111

Fax: (407) 397-8845
Hours: 9:30 am - 7 PM
Description: Explore over 60 of China's most famous landmarks. Enjoy a variety of outstanding entertainment, cuisine and shopping.
Discount: Complimentary admission for Travel Agents and 10% discount off of gate price for their guests. All Travel Agents must check in at guest services with current IATA card and preprinted business card.

Gatorland
14501 S Orange Blossom Trail
Orlando, FL 32837
Tel: (407) 855-5496
Hours: 9 am - dusk
Description: Pure outdoor fun, Gatorland is a laid back day of laughter, amazement, nature and intrigue.
Discount: Agent free admission and 20% off for up to 6 guests. Must present photo ID and leave business card. Accepted year round.

Kennedy Space Center Visitor Complex
Mail Code DNPS
Kennedy Space Center, FL 32899
Tel: (321) 449-4400
Fax: (321) 449-4480
Hours: 9 am - dusk
Description: Tour Kennedy Space Center, meet a real astronaut at the new astronaut encounter show. See the awesome Apollo/Saturn V Center, IMAX space films and mission artifacts.
Discount: One travel agent and two guests receive free bus tour and IMAX movie. Must present IATA card and photo ID. Accepted year round.

Sea World Adventure Park Orlando
7007 Sea World Drive
Orlando, FL 32821
Tel: (407) 363-2200 or toll free 1-800-327-2424
Fax: (407) 363-2255
Hours: Open at 9 am, closing time varies by season
Description: Interactive marine adventure park. New floorless roller coaster KRACKEN, up-close animal encounters and unexpected water-coaster thrills of Journey to Atlantis!
Discount: Agent and one guest receive 50% off. Must present IATA card or embossed business card & photo ID. Accepted year round.

Universal Studios Orlando/ Islands of Adventure

1000 Universal Studios Plaza
Orlando, FL 32819
Tel: (407) 224-6735 or 1-877-UESCAPE
Fax: (407) 224-6735
Hours: Open daily at 9 am, closing times vary
Description: Ride the Movies at the number one movie studio and theme park in the world or Journey through five fantastic islands challenging you to live the adventure.
Discount: Agent receives free admission to both parks w/ up to 6 guests $2.50 off. Must present photo ID & embossed business card. Accepted year round.

Walt Disney World Attractions
PO Box 10,020
Lake Buena Vista, FL 32830
Tel: (407) 397-6551
Fax: (407) 397-6559
US based travel agents requesting discounts must call for an order form: 1-800-900-8080 and request document #121. International travel agents fax request for document #121. Advance notice of 21 days required to process request. Only full-time retail travel agents will qualify. Not offered to traveling companions or family members. Agents are eligible for one 1-day 4-park pass per calendar year.

Water Mania
6073 W Irlo Bronson Hwy
Kissimmee, FL 34746
Tel: (407) 396-2626 ext. 111
Fax: (407) 396-8125
Hours: March - October open daily
Description: 36-acre family water park with heated pool during the winter months. Great group rates and fun for everyone, youth, sports, high school bands, family reunion and church etc.
Discount: Agent free and up to 6 guests rate $12.95. Must present embossed business card & IATA card.

Wet n Wild
6200 International Drive
Orlando, FL 32819
Tel: (407) 351-1800
Fax: (407) 363-1147
Hours: Open daily year-round, hours vary
Description: The Nation's best-attended water park, offers the best variety of multi-passenger water rides in the Orlando area. Something

for everyone and kids can't help but enjoy the elaborate children's playground.
Discount: Instate Agent: Agent receives 50% off and up to 5 guests $5 off. Must present embossed business card & IATA card.
Out-of-state Agent: Agent receives free admission with up to 5 guests $5 off. Must present embossed business card & IATA card.

UNEXPECTED ORLANDO

Astronaut Hall of Fame
6225 Vectorspace Blvd.
Titusville, FL 32780
Tel: (321) 269-6100
Fax: (321) 267-3970
Hours: 9 am - 5 PM
Description: Suit up, strap down, and blast off into an interactive experience that gives you a true taste of space.
Discount: Complimentary admission for agent and one guest. 50% off additional guests in party. Must present photo ID and IATA card.

Harry P. Leu Gardens
1920 North Forest Ave.
Orlando, FL 32803
Tel: (407) 246-2620
Fax: (407) 246-2849
Hours: Monday - Saturday 9 am - 6 PM and Sunday 9 am 5 PM
Daylight Savings Time: Monday - Saturday 9 am - 8 PM and Sunday 9 am - 6 PM
Description: Stroll a 50-acre botanical garden featuring over 2,000 camellias. Visit the Leu House Museum, a national landmark.
Discount: Agents receive free admission with valid IATA card.

Mennello Museum of American Folk Art
900 E. Princeton St.
Orlando, FL 32803
Tel: (407) 246-4278
Fax: (407) 246-4329
Hours: Tuesday - Saturday 11 am - 5 PM (Thursday 11 am - 8 PM), and Sunday noon - 5 PM
Description: Florida's only folk art museum, features paintings by Earl Cunningham, City of Orlando's folk art collection, traveling exhibits, and museum store.
Discount: Free admission for travel agent with IATA card.

Note: IATA card is different from IATAN card. The Anton Anderssen Travel ID card is usually accepted when companies ask for an IATA card.

I recommend having a car while in Orlando, in order to freely visit all the many attractions easily. Unlike Honolulu or New York City, where there's no place to park a car, Orlando has easy and convenient parking almost everywhere. You can ask the tour operator to book an air, hotel, and car as a package, that way the guest gets the huge volume-related rates only a tour operator can provide. Delta Vacations, Disney Travel, Future Vacations, and Funjet are our biggest tour operators for Orlando. One call to the tour operator does it all, including theme park admission tickets.

Arabian Nights
Dinner Attraction
Orlando, Florida

World's Most Honored Dinner Show
* The most beautiful horses in the world.
* Excellent food with unlimited beer & wine each meal.
* Free VIP upgrade for clients of THOR agents
  $15 per guest upgrade includes priority seating, an opportunity to meet the performers and horses in an intimate setting, stable tour, and much more.

* * *

25% Commission + FREE VIP Upgrade
(800) 553-6116
www.arabian-nights.com/Thor

When you book Arabian Nights, be sure to use CLIA number 00 56 1971 to get commission.

TRANSPORTATION

I-Ride Trolley Service
7081 Grand National Drive, #104
Orlando, FL 32819
Tel: (407) 248-9590
Fax: (407) 248-9594
Hours: 7 days a week from 7 am to midnight
Description: I-RIDE is the exclusive transportation service with¡
International Drive area.
Discount: Complimentary three day pass to each qualified t
agent visiting the Orlando area. Maximum of two per trip.
present IATA card.

VIP Limo & Transportation Inc.
1127 Lake Learo Ct.
Orlando, FL 32835
Tel: (407) 822-7755
Fax: (407) 297-1339
Hours: 24 hours a day, 7 days a week
Description: Luxury limousine and shuttle van services speciali
in leisure and group transport to airports, attractions and di
shows.
Discount: Agent receives 15% off any limousine rental or tran
Must present photo ID and business card.

DINNER THEATERS

Pirate's Dinner Adventure
6400 Carrier Drive
Orlando, FL 32819
Tel: (407) 248-0590 or 1-800-866-2469
Fax: (407) 248-0507
Hours: Doors open at 6:30 pm; show starts at 7:45 pm
Description: Visit Orlando's newest treasure. Featuring exciting
performances, daring stunts, musical entertainment and a pira
feast. This adventure has something for everyone. You'll also wan
stay for the Pirate's Buccaneer Bash after the show.
Discount: 50% discount for travel agents and up to six guests. M
present identification, business card and IATA card. Advaı
reservations required contact Greg Calloway or Peg Heinfling.

Alaska

The last frontier

    We book our Alaska tours through Alaska 4 Seasons. Visit them on the web at http://www.alaska4seasons.com/contact.htm Alaska 4 Seasons 4821 E. 115th Avenue/B, Anchorage, Alaska 99516 Phone: (907) 346-1270 Fax: (907) 346-1029 info@alaska4seasons.com Ask for Brigitte. She seems to be the most knowlegable tour operator in Anchorage. This company quotes prices "net." That means no commission is figured in yet. You are absolutely required to add at least 10 percent commission to the package price even if this is for yourself, as a term and condition for using Anton Anderssen Travel's licenses. Failure to do so is fraudulent.
    There are 2 ways of seeing Alaska. One is to take a cruise. They usually start in Seattle, go to Vancouver (foreign ships with foreign employees can't serve US ports unless it's part of an international voyage), then head up the "marine highway" close to the Kenai Peninsula, which is about 2 hours south of Anchorage. If your customer is looking for natural beauty, this is the best option. If your customer is looking for culture, history, shopping, or museums, then a land tour is the best option. They would fly into Anchorage and take day trips to the glaciers, ride on the Alaska Railway, see Denali National Park (Mount McKinley), go to dinner shows, shop at the downtown flea market on the weekends, buy fur coats at discounted rates, visit Eskimo or Native American cultural centers, take trolley tours around town, buy souvenirs at Wal-Mart, K-Mart, and so forth. If they are shoppers, a cruise is a waste of time. If they want great food, then they need to take a cruise. The hotels in Anchorage are very expensive, so a cruise is cheaper from an accommodations viewpoint. The food is a much better value on a cruise. Dining in Anchorage is expensive, but an important restaurant to dine at is Arctic Road Runner Hamburgers (downtown by the creek, 5300 Old Seward Highway). A fun day excursion is taking the Alaska Railroad to the Kenai Fjords National Park, with buffet on Fox Island. Also spectacular is the 26 glacier cruise in Whittier. To get to Whittier you must pass through the Anton Anderson Tunnel. http://www.dot.state.ak.us/creg/whittiertunnel/history.htm

Car Rentals

You must book commissionable rates for customers and yourself. You cannot have travel agent rates for yourself until you have earned your Travel Agent ID card

Whenever a customer needs a car rental, be sure to ask questions such as ages of drivers. Some rental companies will not rent to drivers under 25. The renter also must have a true credit card in most instances. A debit card is not honored for rentals at most rental car companies. Make sure to have the customer sign up for the express rental programs offered by the companies so they can stand in the short line at the rental desk. Also make sure the rental car company is told the airline frequent flyer number for the customer

Advantage Rent-A-Car
http://www.a4ta.com

Alamo
http://www.ta.alamo.com
(800) 327-9633 Reservations
(954) 527-4758 Fax

Auto Europe
http://www.autoeurope.com

Avis
http://www.avisagent.com
Attn. Commission Services
300 Centre Point Drive
Garden City, NY 11530
(800) 522-AVIS

Budget Rent A Car Corporation
http://www.budget.com
http://www.unlimitedbudget.com
4225 Naperville Road, IL 60532
(800) 527-0700 General Reservations
(800) 435-7100 Travel Agent Help
(800) 621-2844 Sales
(800) 842-5628 Meetings
(800) 621-2844 Customer Relations
(630) 955-1900 World Headquarters
(630) 955-7799 Fax

DER Travel Services Europe
http://www.dertravel.com/
car@dertravel.com
9501 West Devon Avenue, Suite 301
Rosemont, IL 60018
(800) 717-4247 - Air Reservations
(800) 782-4248 - All Other Reservations
(888) 712-5727 - Fax Reservations

Dollar Rent A Car
http://www.dollarcar.com/
6th Floor
100 N. Sepulveda Boulevard
El Sequendo, CA 90245
(800) 527-7752
(918) 669-3205 Fax

Hertz
http://www.hertzagent.com
Corp. Sales Office
World Headquarters
(405) 280-6402
(405) 290-2667 Fax
LLiles@hertz.com

Kemwel Holiday Autos LLC.
http://www.kemwel.com/
kha@kemwel.com
106 Calvert Street
Harrison, NY 10528
(800) 678-0678
(914) 825-3150 Fax

National
http://www.nationalcar.com/
7700 France Avenue S.
Minneapolis, MN 55435
(800) 627-7777
(612) 893-6386 Fax

Payless
http://www.paylesscarrental.com

Thrifty
http://www.thrifty.com/
P.O. Box 26120
Tulsa, OK 74153-0250
(800) 822-8257
(800)367-2277
(918) 669-2180 Fax

Value Rent-A-Car
(800) 468-2583

Some cities are over crowded and you should advise the customer not to rent a car while there. Those places include Honolulu, New York City, downtown Chicago, French Quarter in New Orleans, most cities in Europe, and most cities in Mexico.

The cheapest rental car companies for vacation customers tend to be Alamo and Avis. Make sure you tell the customer to put gas back in the car when renting, even if they drive the car only 5 miles, because many companies charge a fee for not doing so, even when it's obvious there was no need to.

If your customer overstays the rental period, there is a nasty fee to pay. It's better to guess in favor of a longer stay than needed when the customer is unsure how many days he needs. Once he picks up the car, he can't extend the rental period without incurring these fees.

Travel

Cruise Lines

Cruises are the best value for your customer's vacation dollar

Cruise lines usually ask for the agency phone number to look up Anton Anderssen Travel in their computer. Be certain to ask questions about all fees the customer must pay, including cruise fare, taxes, port charges, airport fees, air taxes, and any other hidden costs. Also be sure to distinguish between the gross price and the net price. The gross price is what the customer is required to pay. If you don't collect the gross price from the customer and pass it on to the cruise line, Anton Anderssen Travel will refuse to give the documents to you. The customer must pay the gross price. The gross price minus commission is the net. You are not allowed to give the net price to the customer, even if it for yourself, because that means Anton Anderssen Travel will receive no commission for the booking.

When you make a reservation, the cruise line will usually give you the choice between "cabin assignment" or "category guarantee." Cabin Assignment means your customer is assigned to a particular room from day 1. "Category Guarantee" is the best value for your customer. It means they will get at least the category type room they are paying for, but 75% of the time they usually will get a free upgrade when they show up for the cruise.

Customers must have proof of citizenship to get on cruises. That means a passport or birth certificate with raised seal and driver's license.

Customers choose early dining or late dining. Late dining allows more time during the day to go on excursions. Early diners might be rushed out of the shows to make room for the second show that the later diners are coming to. Early dining will have more kids in the room.

Most cruises have free room service. That means your customer can order hamburgers, pizza, and other short-order menu items 24 hours a day by calling room service on the cabin phone.

Soft drinks are usually free only at dinner. Otherwise the customer has to pay for the drinks. Some cruises allow the customer to get a drink pass which is good all week for unlimited beverages.

If you let the cruise line write the airline tickets for your customer, then transfers from the airport to the cruise port are free.

If the customer is traveling during bad weather, they can do a "deviation." That means they fly into the port city a few days early, or a few days after the cruise. It's best to fly in a day or two early to make sure to get on the boat. In the event of a bad snowstorm, flights could be delayed or cancelled and the customer could miss the boat if he doesn't get to the port in time. Getting there a day early makes best sense during snowstorm season. This is really important if the cruise is overseas.

There is usually a fee to do an air deviation. The cruise line will write your tickets, reserve a hotel during the deviation, then provide transfers to the port in most cases.

If you are booking a group, you have to keep track of each cabin individually as far as how much each cabin has paid, and what each cabin owes. You can't just ask the cruise line "How much do we owe?" because they will tell you the net price (gross minus commission). If you don't collect the full gross price from your customers for every cabin, you won't get your cruise documents until the gross amount is paid in full.

American West Steamboat Co.
Two Union Square
601 Union Street
Suite 4343
Seattle, WA 98101
(206) 292-9606
(800) 434-1232 Reservations

Carnival Cruise Lines
http://www.carnival.com/
3655 N.W. 87 Avenue
Miami, FL 33178
(305) 599-2600
(800) 327-9501 Reservations
(800) 327-5782 Groups

Celebrity Cruises
http://www.celebrity-cruises.com/
5201 Blue Lagoon Drive
Miami, FL 33126
(305) 967-2110
(800) 437-3111 Reservations
(800) 437-4111 Groups

Clipper Cruise Line
http://www.clippercruise.com/
7711 Bonhomme Avenue
St. Louis, MO 63105
(314) 727-2929
(800) 325-0010
(314) 727-6576 Fax

Costa Cruises
World Trade Center
80 S.W. 8th Street
Miami, FL 33130
(305) 358-7325
(800) 462-6782 Reservations

Crystal Cruises
2121 Avenue of the Stars
Los Angeles, CA 90067
(310) 785-9300
(800) 446-6620 Reservations

Cunard Line
http://www.cunardline.com/
555 Fifth Avenue
New York, NY 10017
(212) 880-7500
(800) 528-6273 Reservations
(800) 221-4770

Delta Queen Steamboat Co.
http://www.deltaqueen.com/
Robin Street Wharf
1380 Port of New Orleans
(504) 586-0631
(800) 543-1949 Reservations
(800) 458-6789 Groups

Disney Cruise Line
http://www.disney.com/DisneyCruise
210 Celebration Place

Suite 4000
Celebration, FL 34747
(407) 827-8473

First European Cruises
http://www.first-european.com
95 Madison Avenue
New York, NY 10016
(888) 983-8767

Holland America Line
http://www.hollandamerica.com/
300 Elliott Avenue West
Seattle, WA 98119
(206) 281-3535
(800) 426-0327

Ivaran Lines
Newport Financial Center
111 Pavonia Avenue
Jersey City, NJ 07310-1755
(201) 798-5656
(800) 451-1639

MSC Italian Cruises
http://www.msccruisesusa.com
420 Fifth Avenue
New York, NY 10018
(800) 666-9333

Norwegian Coastal Voyages
http://www.coastalvoyage.com/
bo.fridsberg@Coastalvoyage.com
405 Park Avenue
New York, NY 10022
(212) 319-1300
(800) 323-7436 Reservations

Norwegian Cruise Line
http://www.ncl.com/
95 Merrick Way
Coral Gables, FL 33134
(305) 447-9660
(800) 333-7300

Nubian Nile Cruises
http://www.nubiannilecruises.com/
kingtut916@aol.com
1255 Post St. #506
San Francisco, CA 94109
(888) 466-8242
(415) 398-2176 Fax

Orient Lines
1510 S.E. 17th Street
Suite 4000
Fort Lauderdale, FL 33316

(954) 527-6660
(800) 333-7300

Princess Cruises
http://www.princesscruises.com/
10100 Santa Monica Boulevard
Suite 1800
Los Angeles, CA 90067
(310) 553-1770
(800) 421-0522

Radisson Seven Seas Cruises
600 Corporate Drive
Suite 410
Fort Lauderdale, FL 33334
(305) 776-6123
(800) 333-3333

Regal Cruises
http://www.regalcruises.com/
4199 34th Street
Suite B103
St. Petersburg, FL 33711
(813) 867-7107
(800) 270-7245

Royal Caribbean International
http://www.royalcaribbean.com/
1050 Carribean Way
Miami, FL 33132-2096
(305) 539-6000
(800) 327-6700 Reservations
(800) 327-2055 Groups

Royal Olympic Cruise Lines
http://www.epirotiki.com/
One Rockerfeller Plaza
Suite 315
New York, NY 10020
(212) 397-6400
(800) 872-6400

Seabourn Cruise Line
http://www.seabourn.com
6100 Blue Lagoon Dr.
Miami, FL 33126
(800) 929-9391

SITA World Travel, Inc.
http://www.sitatours.com/
sitatours@sitatours.com
16250 Ventura Boulevard
Suite # 300
Encino, CA 91436
(800) 421-5643
(818) 990-9762 Fax

We currently book STAR Cruises in the Orient.

Star Clippers
http://www.starclippers.com/
4101 Salzedo Avenue
Coral Gables, FL 33146
(305) 442-0550
(800) 442-0551

Windjammer Barefoot Cruises
http://www.windjammer.com/
P.O. Box 190120
Miami Beach, FL 33119-0120
(305) 672-6453
(800) 327-2602

Windstar Cruises
http://www.windstarcruises.com/
300 Elliott Avenue West
Seattle, WA 98119
(206) 281-3535
(800) 258-7245

World Explorer Cruises
http://www.wecruise.com/
info@wecruise.com
555 Montgomery Street
Suite 1400
San Francisco, CA. 94111-2544
415-820-9200
415-820-9292 Fax
800-854-3835 Reservations
800-325-2752   Brochure   Hot-Line

CLIA CRUISE ACADEMY

www.cruising.org

Becoming A CLIA Certified Cruise Counsellor is Easier Than You Think:

Enroll in the Program. Complete the application on the reverse side. In 2 weeks, you'll receive your enrollment materials.

Determine Credit Already Earned. Credit is awarded for items completed and product knowledge within the past 3 years. (see credit requirements charts). Order exams for training programs already attended and videos you already have.

Earn Remaining Credits & Certification Within 2 Years. You have 2 years from date of enrollment to achieve ACC Certification (and 2 additional years for MCC) by fulfilling credit requirements. Submit your completed Captain's Log with the appropriate documentation for your Certified Cruise Counsellor material!

ACCREDITED CRUISE COUNSELLOR REQUIREMENTS (ACC)
100 Total Credits

A. Mandatory Training (30 credits)
- Completion of 2 CLIA Classroom or Online Courses & Exams (15 credits each) - OR -
- Completion of "Cruising—A Guide To The Cruise Industry" Textbook & exam (30 credits)

B. Any Combination of Elective Training (50 credits)
- Completion of Other CLIA Training Seminars and Exams (15 credits each)
- Completion of CLIA Video Training and Exams (10 credits each)
- Attendance at CLIA Co-Sponsored/Endorsed Cruise Conferences (10 credits per event)
- Completion of CLIA Institute (50 credits per Institute)
- Completion of "Cruising—A Guide To The Cruise Industry" Textbook & exam (30 credits)
- Achievement of ICTA's CTC or CTA designation (10 credits)
- Attendance at member line product seminars (2 credits ea. max. 10 credits)
- Achievement of CITC's CTC or CTM designation (10 credits)

C. Product Knowledge (20 credits) (CLIA Member Cruise Lines only)
- Personal Cruise Experience (5 credits per cruise) 10 credits required:
  One cruise of 2-6 days, one cruise of 7+ days, both on different CLIA member lines
- Shipboard Inspections (2 credits per ship) 10 credits required

---

MASTER CRUISE COUNSELLOR REQUIREMENTS (MCC)
100 Total Credits (In addition to ACC Requirements)

A. Mandatory Training (50 credits)
- Successful Completion of 3 Case Studies (50 total credits) - OR -
- Successful Completion of CLIA Institute (50 credits)

B. Any Combination of Elective Training (30 credits)
- Completion of Other CLIA Training Seminars and Exams (15 credits each)
- Completion of CLIA Video Training and Exams (10 credits each)
- Attendance at CLIA Co-sponsored/Endorsed Cruise Conferences (10 credits each)
- Completion of "Cruising—A Guide To The Cruise Industry" Textbook and exam (30 credits)
- Achievement of ICTA's CTC or CTA designation (10 credits)
- Attendance at member line product seminars (2 credits ea. max. 10 credits)
- Achievement of CITC's CTC or CTM designation (10 credits)

C. Product Knowledge (CLIA Member Cruise Lines only) (20 credits)
- Personal Cruise Experience (5 credits per cruise) 10 credits required:
  One cruise of 2-6 days, one cruise of 7+ days, on any CLIA member line ships
- Shipboard Inspections (2 credits per ship) 10 credits required

Disney Cruise Line

Travel Industry Reduced Rate Offers and Procedures

Space Available Offer

Passengers	3-Night Cruise 1-2	3-4	4-Night Cruise 1-2	3-4	7-Night Cruise 1-2	3-4
CLIA Agents	$249.00 per person	$149.00 per person	$299.00 per person	$179.00 per person	$499.00 per person	$249.00 per person
Non-CLIA Agents	$299.00 per person	$149.00 per person	$399.00 per person	$179.00 per person	$699.00 per person	$249.00 per person

For Space Available requests, please call *Disney Cruise Line®* at **407-566-6967**, between the hours of 8:00 a.m. - 10:00 p.m. EST Monday - Friday and 9:00 a.m. - 8:00 p.m. EST Saturday and Sunday. Please call <u>no more than 30</u> days prior to sailing date.

Within 24 hours of confirmation, please submit verification by mail or fax to:

Disney Cruise Vacations
Attention: Inventory Control
P.O. Box 10100
Lake Buena Vista, Florida 32830-0020
Fax: 407-566-7739

Proper forms of verification include the following:

- A current photocopy of the agency's IATA list, or agent's IATAN card.
- A CLIA ID card or current copy of the agency's CLIA certificate along with a letter of approval from the agency's owner/manager.

Tour Operators

Remember that the huge vendors have huge buying power, offering huge savings

They say things are cheaper by the dozen. Well if that's true, then it's certainly cheaper by the thousand. Tour operators negotiate for thousands of airline tickets, hotel nights, and car rentals. They bundle the items together, then pass the savings on to you. Let's say you wanted to stay 5 nights in Hawaii. It would be a whole lot cheaper to get a 5 night land package from Pleasant Hawaiian Holidays for hotel x than it would be to call hotel x and book 5 nights for a client. You always want to go through huge volume vendors to hook on to their buying power. If you know a customer wants a particular hotel, you can call that hotel and ask the sales office "Which tour operators have booking space at your hotel?" then call the tour operator and book through them. You'll probably get a better commission too.

Each vendor has its own way of storing travel agency information into their computers. Some vendors use the CLIA license, others the ARC license, others the IATA license, others the agency telephone number, others a unique number. You will need to know how a vendor has the agency listed in their computer before calling them to make a reservation, otherwise the reservations department might not be able to find our agency. The default account number when a supplier cannot find our agency is the ARC number: 53 40 2591.

My favorite Tour Operators are Apple, Funjet, Blue Sky Tours, America West Vacations, DER, GoWay, and Delta Dream Vacations. Be sure to look at http://www.TravelAgentCollege.com for updates.

Commissionable means the vendor will pay a certain amount of what the customer spends to the licensed agency as a reward for finding the customer.

Only commissionable sales count toward your credentials. If you book net rates you must add commission. Until you earned your CLIA ID card you are not entitled to travel agent rates / discounts. If you book travel agent discounts before you earn the CLIA card, the agency will instruct the vendor to cancel out your reservation, and you will not receive a refund of any kind due to the fraud involved. Commissions are split between the agency and the agent (you). You are an independent contractor, not an employee. Your contract will be terminated at the first incidence of any fraud.

Until you earn your CLIA "Travel Agent ID" credentials, you are a reservation service provider, and an intern at an agency. You may book travel under our agency's licenses to gain experience and credit towards your credentials, but you yourself are not yet entitled to the travel agent rates until you EARN the credentials. You may never circumvent adding commission onto a "net" fare by sending only the "net" amount to a vendor. It must be net plus at least 10%, even if the travel is for yourself.

Get your free business cards from http://www.vistaprint.com/frf?frf=542155973501
All you have to do is pay for shipping. Your card should resemble something like this:

Your Name Here
Reservation Service Associate

Anton Anderssen Travel
Independent Affiliate
Agency: 4177 Garrick Ave, Warren MI 48091
Agency Phone 586 757 4177
Home Phone Here
Your Email Here
www.GeoCities.com/YahooID

Anton Anderssen Travel

Passenger Profile

This information will enable us to better serve our valued customers!

Mail to: Anton Anderssen Travel, 4177 Garrick Av, Warren MI 48091

Passenger Profile

Agent Name: _____
Passenger Last Name: _____
Passenger First Names: _____
Street Address: _____
City, State, ZIP: _____
Telephone: _____
Email Address: _____
Best time to call: _____
Ages of Adults: _____
Ages of Children under 18: _____
Is everyone traveling a US Citizen?: ☐ Yes ☐ No Passport #: _____
I am interested in: ☐ Cruise ☐ Family ☐ Romance ☐ FIT/Indpt ☐ Esc Tour

Supplier Info

Supplier: _____
Res Agent name: _____
Res Agent sine: _____
Rec Loc: _____
Deposit $ _____ Date: _____
Final Payment $ _____ Date: _____
Docs in / Payment Frm / Comm _____

Make sure the supplier has the customer name correct. Don't pay the supplier any money until you see a confirmation showing the name spelled correctly. If it is a cruise, and they have the name incorrect, tell them to change the computer record without re-issuing documents if the documents have already been issued. You must use the name on the customer's driver's license.

Cruise Vacation Profile

Do you need airfare?: ☐ yes ☐ no

If yes, from which departure city?: _____

Is this a special occasion?: ☐ Wedding ☐ Anniv. ☐ Birthday ☐ Other Date _____

What type of stateroom do you want?: ☐ Inside ☐ Outside ☐ Balcony ☐ MiniSuite ☐ Suite

Category Guarantee? ☐ yes (might get upgraded) ☐ no (stateroom # assigned) Smoking?: ☐ yes ☐ no

Cabin occupancy: ☐ Single ☐ Double ☐ Triple ☐ Quad ☐ Quint

Seating Preference: ☐ Early ☐ Late   Departure date _____ Return date _____

Table size?: ☐ 2 ☐ 4 ☐ 6 ☐ 8 ☐ 10 ☐ I don't care

If Caribbean, which itinerary: ☐ Eastern (shopping) ☐ Western (sun & sand) ☐ Southern (exotic)

Ship Name: _____ Stateroom Category: _____

Cruised / Toured with this company before?: ☐ yes ☐ no   Trip Insurance?: ☐ yes ☐ no

Dietary needs: ☐ Low fat ☐ Diabetic ☐ Kosher ☐ Vegetarian ☐ Low Salt

What are the ages of the guests?: _____

Specific Needs: _____

Pre or Post Cruise Packages: _____

	Passenger 1	Passenger 2	Passenger 3+
Cruise / Tour cost			
Air add on			
Port charges			
Ship Gov Taxes			
Pre cruise tour			
Post cruise tour			
Insurance			
Transfers			
Air Taxes			
Total Cost			

Option date _____

Deposit   Date _____   Amt _____   Payment type _____
Deposit   Date _____   Amt _____   Payment type _____
Final Payment Date _____ Amt _____ Payment type _____
Cancellation policy _____ Payment type _____

Taxes and port charges are sometimes called "non commissionable fares." This can be confusing. Be certain you write down the Gross amount, because that is what you have to collect from the guest. The cruise lines indicate "amount due" on confirmations but that is not the amount due from the customer. That's the amount due to the cruise line after subtracting the commission, also known as NET. You can't collect just the net – you must collect the gross and know the difference.

Air/Hotel Air/Car or Tour Vacation Profile

Ages of Adults:

Do you need a rental car?: ☐ yes ☐ no

If yes, which size car?: _____

Do you need a hotel?: ☐ yes ☐ no

If yes, which chain?: _____

Type of Hotel: ☐ Budget ☐ Moderate ☐ 1st Class ☐ Deluxe ☐ All Incl

Do you wish to purchase Travel Insurance??: ☐ yes ☐ no

Is there any info that will help us plan your vacation?:

Places you enjoyed before: ☐ Alaska   ☐ Florida / Disney   ☐ Caribbean
                           ☐ Europe   ☐ Las Vegas   ☐ Mexico

Always quote insurance in the price for your customer. You can always remove it if the customer does not want it. Assume they do. You never know when there is going to be a death in the family and the passengers try to get their thousands of dollars back.

I HAVE READ AND UNDERSTAND THE ABOVE RESERVATION AND IT ACCURATELY REFLECTS WHAT WAS REQUESTED. I UNDERSTAND THAT I AM STRONGLY ENCOURAGED TO PURCHASE TRAVEL INSURANCE.

CLIENT SIGNATURE _____ DATE _____

With my signature, I the Traveler have approved the use of the above information for my travel needs. This also authorizes the use of credit card number(s), when traveling on business or pleasure. This signed form will remain on file at Anton Anderssen Travel, the Authorized Travel Agency

Credit Card _____ Type _____ # _____ Expiry _____

Name as printed on card _____

Billing address of cardholder _____

If credit card holder is not the lead name of traveler, relationship to traveler _____

Phone numbers of client _____

CLIENT SIGNATURE _____ DATE _____

It is very important to get the customer to give written permission to use their charge card, and to approve the tour or cruise reservation order. If you don't get a customer signature and the customer does a charge back on their credit card, you are responsible for paying the bill, even if it's thousands of dollars. Don't risk a verbal OK… get authorization in writing from the customer.

Anton Anderssen Travel

IATA License 52 43 1875

Usually used for international travel

CLIA license 00 56 1971

Usually used with cruises

ARC license 53 40 2591

This is the most important license. Whenever you call a supplier and they do not have us listed in their database, tell them to use this ARC number, as opposed to IATA or CLIA or other account numbers.

4177 Garrick Av, Warren Mi 48091

Never tell the supplier YOUR address as the agency address because everyone's documents will start going to your house

http://www.TravelAgentCollege.com/
(tours, hotels, cruises, packages, cars)

http://travel.isWonderful.com
http://www.WeTravelFree.com

(today's specials from dozens of suppliers)

email: Anton@AntonTravel.com

To reach Anton call toll free 1 866 825 5286 then enter the agency phone number 586 757 4177

The agency fax number is 313 557 6367

73
BOOKING IS EASY

Just call the supplier and give the following info:

- Hello, my name is _____ . I am an associate from Anton Anderssen Travel.
- I would like to make a reservation that is commissionable to Anton Anderssen Travel. Our IATA number is 52 43 1875 (or CLIA number is 00 56 1971 or ARC number is 53 40 2591) (You have to look at the descriptions for each individual supplier to know in advance exactly which number they are seeking in their computer system)
- Our agency phone number is 586 757 4177 (never give them any different #)
- Our agency fax is 313 557 6367
- I would like to make a reservation for John Doe at _____ hotel / cruise ship / vacation package on (date) for ____ nights
- There are _____ number of people in the room / cabin
- They want _____ beds (king, 2 queens, 2 twins, etc)
- Smoking / Non smoking
- Airfare is needed from Detroit (or wherever)
- What commission amount will you be paying for this booking??
- What is the confirmation number?

Important rule: If this booking is for yourself or your family, never ask the supplier to give you personally a "travel industry employee rate" or "Travel Agents Only" rate or "Discount exclusively for Travel Agents" until you earn your travel agent credentials ($1,250 in earned commissions) otherwise you are committing fraud, because until you earn your credentials you are not a *bona fide* travel agent yet, you are just an associate. You can still take advantage of other bargains and discounts available to the general public, for example, the public specials at **http://WeTravelFree.com** or AAA rates, or senior citizen rates, or any other promotion priced for people OTHER THAN rates exclusively given to Travel Agents for personal travel. Management reserves the right to cancel all bookings made fraudulently.

Example: Sheraton offers a hotel room. The price for the same room varies according to the rate you select for your customer: Rack Rate $100, Weekend Rate $69, AARP Rate $50, Manager's Special $49, Internet Rate $55, AAA rate $64, Two for Breakfast Rate $70, Military Rate $50, Government Rate $60, Corporate Rate $65, Sam's Club Members Rate $49, Entertainment Coupon Rate $50, Travel Agent Rate $39. You are allowed to book any of these rates (provided the customer qualifies), but you may NEVER book the "Travel Agent Rate" for any customers, and you may NEVER book the "Travel Agent Rate" for yourself until you earned your Travel Agent ID Card. Do not break this rule under any condition, because you will not be forgiven, you will be prosecuted.

You usually don't get commission when you buy directly from an airline, because most airlines don't pay commissions on public airfares (exceptions are SpiritAir.com, USA3000, AirTran, and charters). You can go through a tour operator who will give you a commissionable air and hotel or car package. It is assumed that if the customer only wants published airfare from a scheduled carrier (as opposed to a charter) they are smart enough to call the airline themselves. You still get commission on charters or packaged airfare or consolidators.

Then tell the customer the price (also known as rate or tariff) and his confirmation number. The supplier will pay us after the guest finishes the vacation, and you will get credit toward a travel agent ID (giving you lots of fun discounts) plus 50 to 70 percent of the commission paid by the tour operator.

TRAVEL AGENT Discounts are only for agents who have EARNED their travel agent ID, otherwise you are still entitled to the fantastic PUBLIC rates offered at http://www.WeTravelFree.com or any other PUBLIC rate offered to the general public.

After you have earned $1,250 in commissions you will earn an official CLIA-issued Travel Agent ID card. This card is honored by cruise lines for travel agent discount rates as low as $35 per day on cruises!

Cards are valid for the CALENDAR year, always expiring Dec 31. There is an $18 processing fee payable to CLIA. For inquiries regarding the status of your CLIA card application, call 603 629 0820. Fax 413 637 5400.

It is very important that travel interns / travel agent associates NEVER change the address, fax number, phone, password, etc. for the Anton Anderssen Travel account with any supplier. If any of an associate's information is discovered on file with a supplier under the Anton Anderssen Travel account number, a $100 fee will be assessed. This fee includes but is not limited to: changing the agency address, phone, fax, internet password or Tour Source access. This fee is also applicable for having documents sent directly to an associate/client via online bookings. This fee is NON-REFUNDABLE. Never tell a supplier that Anton Anderssen Travel is located at your personal address or phone number unless you are willing to pay a $100 fee every time you do so. All documents and information MUST flow through Anton Anderssen Travel's proper address.

When you book a vacation for a customer you need to send your booking information to Anton@AntonTravel.com so you can get your commission and so we know to send the documents to you. We need this information:
- o   Passenger names
- o   Address of passengers
- o   Phone numbers of passengers
- o   Dates of Travel
- o   Destination
- o   Booking # (confirmation #)
- o   Tour operator's name / supplier's name
- o   Commission amount the tour operator says they will pay
- o   Total amount of the vacation
- o   Is this air-only or is this a package? If package, what hotel or other items are in the package?

Email Account
http://www.wapda.com

You need an email client that will show html documents. The best free email is wapda. AOL is probably the worst email client you can use because it strips out all pictures.

Business Cards
http://www.vistaprint.com

You receive 250 free business cards at http://freecards.AreCool.net Just fill out the blanks and pay for shipping. Hand out your business cards to let everyone know you are now a travel agent. If you are in a hurry, you can create printable business cards online at http://www.jobcards.com

Free Brochures
www.leadnet.com/pubs/cntr.html

www.recommend.com/ai

www.tlexplorer.com

www.orderCaribbean.com

http://www.ordertravelsavers.com/

http://www.orderEurope.com/

www.travelpromotions.com

Go to these sites to select tons of free brochures from cruise lines, tourism bureaus, and more.
    For a free Caribbean Vacation Planner call 800 356 9999 x717

Las Vegas CVB
www.vegasfreedom.com

www.lvcva.com

They will mail out brochures and info. The websites list commissionable travel in Las Vegas. Our contact is John Meyer jmeyer@lvcva.com   Phone: 702 892 0711   Fax: 702 892 2906

Vacation Access
www.vaxvacationaccess.com

Book tons of vacations from different tour operators in 1 convenient web site. Enter agency number 8107574177 ID: Anton Student Password: Anton will give you the password after you have experience booking several funjet packages. (414) 934-2900 vax tech support. vaxtechsupport@triseptsolutions.com

Hotels.com
http://Hotels.com/

Go to the website. Click on the TRAVEL AGENTS link (it's toward the bottom of the page in red letters, underneath "Services and Customer Care" Put in our ARC number 53402591

Red Horse Inn Orlando
http://www.RedHorseOrlando.com/

Voice: (407) 351-4100 Fax: (407) 996-4599 Reservations: (877) 936-4100 Located at International Drive and Kirkman Road, this property is colorful, clean, and in a perfect location. Ask for the special "Anton Anderssen Travel" rate of $45, and tell them "make this commissionable to Anton Anderssen Travel, IATA number 52431875" Director of Sales -Kelie Smit

Arabian Nights Orlando
http://www.arabian-nights.com/thor

Reservation Department at 800-553-6116 or locally at 407-239-9223. Ask for the THOR consortium's 25% discount plus free VIP upgrade for your customers. Tell them to make this commissionable to Anton Anderssen Travel under CLIA number 00 56 1971

Marriott Hotels
http://www.Marriott.com/

800 831 1000 Courtyard, Residence Inn, Fairfield, Marriott, Spring Hill Suites, Towne Place Suites, Marriott, Renaissance, New World International, Ramada International properties, Ritz Carlton, Villa properties. When it asks for an ARC IATA number enter 53 40 2591 Questions about commission to tas.rep@marriott.com.

Hilton Hotels
www.hilton.com

800 Hiltons Use ARC number 53 40 2591 to identify yourself as Anton Anderssen Travel. Hilton, Conrad Hotels, Doubletree, Embassy Suites Hotels, Hampton Inn, Hampton Inn & Suites, Hilton Grand Vacations Club Homewood Suites by Hilton, Harrison Conference Centers, Scandic, Camino Real

Best Western Hotels

http://www.bestwestern.com/

Use Anton Anderssen Travel's account number 00561971 when asked for ID or IATA number.
Telephone: 1-800-780-7234 (Toll Free)
Hearing Impaired: 1-800-528-2222 . Best Western Hotels are Independently owned & operated. It is the largest chain in the world.

Utell Hotels International
http://www.utell.com/

Use Anton Anderssen Travel's account number 00021315 in the IATA box either at the web site or by calling them at 1 800 44 UTELL or 1 800 448 8355

Choice Hotels International ☺
http://www.choicehotels.com

Use Anton Anderssen Travel's CLIA number to book hotel reservations at over 2300 Choice Hotels around the world! Book online (click the link that says "Travel Agent City" on the left column, or call toll free 1 800 4 Choice or 800 228 5050 and give ARC number 53 40 2591 (first initial of agency is R) (or CLIA number 00 56 1971, first initial of agency is A) when they ask for an IATA number. Tell them your customer has a discount code ID# 00 801 318. Reservations in French (800) 267-3837. Spanish (866) 291-9816

- Comfort
- Clarion
- Rodeway
- Quality
- Quality Suites
- Sleep Inn
- Econo Lodge

STARWOOD RESORTS

Use Anton Anderssen Travel CLIA number 00 56 1971 to book Starwood Hotels and Resorts. Call 800 334 8484 Group desk 800 301 1111
- Travel Agent Discounts available
- Includes Sheraton, St. Regis, Westin, Four Points Luxury Collection, W Hotels
- Hotels all over the world

Six Continents Hotels

http://www.sixcontinentshotels.com/holiday-inn
At the website click on the green "Travel Agents" button. Inter-Continental 800 327 0200; Crowne Plaza 800 CROWNE; Holiday Inn 800 HOLIDAY. Use ARC number 53 40 2591 instead of the IATA number.

Swisshotel

International 800 63 SWISS, Domestic USA 800 73 SWISS

Cendant Hotels

Use Anton Anderssen Travel's special CLIA number 00 56 1971 (when they ask for an IATA number) for any of these Cendant Hotels:

- Days Inn 800 DAYS INN
- Howard Johnson 800 4GO HOJO
- Knights Inn 800 843 5644
- Ramada Inn 800 2 RAMADA
- Travelodge 800 578 7878
- Wingate 800 441 1748
- Villager 800 328 7829

- Amerihost 800 434 5800
- Super8   800 800 8000

When booking any of the above-listed hotels, tell the reservations agent you have a discount code of 26146.

When booking Ramada, tell the Reservations operator that your customer has a Ramada discount ID 932962 from "Perks at Work"

Aladdin Hotel Las Vegas
To make reservations, call Aladdin at 877 333 WISH

Bellagio Hotel Las Vegas
To make reservations, call Bellagio at 888 987 6667 and give them Anton Anderssen Travel's account number 757 4177.

Extended Stay America
Travel agent commission of 10% is paid up to the first seven (7) nights of a stay when booked through Call Center (1-800-EXT-STAY) only.

Commission is not payable when reservations are booked through the web site or the property directly. Travel Agents needing assistance with reservations may call the Unirez Customer Help line at 877-920-9199.

Beaches Resorts
http://www.sandals.com/

Ultra all-inclusive resorts in the Caribbean. To make reservations, call Beaches at 800 BEACHES and give them Anton Anderssen Travel's account number 00 56 1971. Our DSM is Melissa Mango or 888 SANDALS.   Email mmango4969@aol.com

Sandals Resorts
http://www.sandals.com/

Ultra all-inclusive resorts in the Caribbean. To make reservations, call Sandals at 888 SANDALS or 800 327

1991 and give them Anton Anderssen Travel's account number 00 56 1971. Our rep: Melissa Mango   Inside Sales Manager: 1-800-327-1991 xt. 277   See current specials at http://content.onlineagency.com/sites/7845/index.asp Toll free 800 48 Special

Wyndham Hotels
http://www.wyndham.com/

Use ARC number 53402591. Reservations 877 999 3223. Travel Agent support 888 799 4747. Fax 972 315 7067.

Contiki Vacations
http://www.contiki.com/

Vacations for 18 to 35 year olds. For brochures, fax request to 714 939 4960 or email brochures@contiki.com

Spirit Airlines ☺

http://www.spiritair.com

800 772 7117 Normally, you can never make air reservations straight from the airline, because they would force you to create the record yourself using a CRS. Anton Anderssen Travel has a contract with Spirit that allows travel agents to make bookings on the web site and still get commission. Go to the website, and click on the option at the left that says "Travel Agents". For ARC number, enter 53 40 2591. Enter 4177 as the last 4 digits of Anton Anderssen Travel's phone number. You should see a page that says "Welcome to the Spirit Airlines Travel Agency Online Reservations." Click on the to and from city, and the dates. Select a departing flight option then click "forward". Then select a returning flight. Click "I agree to the terms" then "forward". You will see a fare breakdown, including the commission amount. If you don't see a commission amount, you are not in travel

agent mode and will not get a commission. For contact information put your full name. For email use Anton@AntonTravel.com and also put the customer's email or your email in the customer email box. Warning: You will be booted out of the travel agent mode (the only way to get commissions) of the website unknowingly if you take more than 15 minutes to do a booking, or if you have to go "back" and change dates a few times or if an incorrect format was entered. While booking the reservation via the website, you may look for things to confirm that you are in the travel agent mode such as in the point of the fare itemized breakdown, the commission total should compute. If you don't see anything about a commission in the fare breakdown, you are not in the travel agent mode. Also, at the end of the record after entering all credit card information, there should be 2 options for an email address: One option for a travel agent itinerary and one option for a passenger itinerary. The last point of verification would be on the travel agent itinerary. It should show the commission amount. If while booking your reservation you notice that you did not see the commission in the record or the 2 options to email the itinerary, please call Denise immediately 586 741 8912 so she can figure out why the commission had not computed. To see where Spirit flies, go to http://www.spiritair.com/routemap.cfm . Spirit offers incredible internet specials, like Florida for $59 each way. These specials can be booked using Anton Anderssen Travel's number, and it will be commissionable. Spirit offers airfare to Denver, LA, Myrtle Beach, NY, DC, Cancun, Las Vegas, Atlantic City, Florida and Puerto Rico. Great for cruise passengers who want to purchase airfare separately. Sales support fax 586 741 8976. Our DSM is Carol Meth 800 246 7688 ext 2500, fax 313 383 0325 CarolM@spiritair.com Spirit Vacations at or 888 205 3315 or 1-800-509-0453. For commission inquiries call Denise Olzewski (800) 772-7117 ext. 8912 or 586 741 8912, fax 586 791 1397. Agent reduced rate phone 800 246 7688 x8989 or fax 586 741 8916. To get seat assignments go to https://www.spiritair.com/Welcome.aspx?pg=bkgModManager

USA 3000 Airlines ☺
http://www.usa3000.com/

Click on "Travel Agents Only" link at the bottom left corner. Use ARC number 53402591. Call 1-877-872-3000 1-877-USA3000 Flies to St Pete and Ft Lauderdale a few times a week. Flight info 800 895 3000 For agent rates, fax 610 325 1535 give name, ARC, provide conf number for flights that you've booked, give contact info, Attn Emile famtrips@usa3000airlines.com fax 610 325 1896

Air Tran ☺
http://www.airtran.com/

Anton Anderssen Travel. Services Flint airport. Click on "Travel Agents" button. Travel Agency ID 00561971 password: lovebug   (all small letters) NEVER CHANGE THIS PASSWORD Commission problems: Virginia Muse 407 251 3627, fax 407 251 3749   AirTran reservations (call in reservations non commissionable)

Superclubs
www.superclubs.com/travel_agents/

877 Go Super or 800 Go Super. Grand Lido Resorts (luxury), Breezes (active), and Hedonism (wicked). Fax (954)925-6975 (954) 925-0334 Give them IATA number 52 43 1875   Contact Steve Howel at 800 467 8737 x 5720 for weblink problems

Club Med
www.clubmed.com

800 CLUB MED. 888 WEB CLUB. Warning: Club med has extra "membership fees" Tell the person answering the phone that they might have to load in the IATA number again because they have a really old computer reservation system that is not up to date with the IATA database. Group desk 800 453 2582. For brochures and display materials fax your request to 313 274 9636.

Freedom Paradise Resort

http://www.freedomparadise.com

For hotel reservations, please call toll free 866 LIVE XXL. The resort for chubby people. Cancun. reservations@freedomparadise.com Tel. +52 (998) 887 1101 Address: Km. 237 Freeway Cancun-Tulum; Tulum, Quintana Roo; México, C.P. 77780

Palace Resorts

http://www.palaceresorts.com/TravelAgents/TravelAgent_Index.asp

ARC number 53402591 For hotel reservations, please call toll free at 1-800-635-1836 Ext. 6030 and someone will be able to assist you in reserving your dream vacation. These are all inclusive resorts, famous in Cancun.

Apple Vacations ☺

http://www.applevacations.com

myappleonline.com

http://www.AppleSpecials.US

To make reservations, go to internet site https://partners.applevacations.com/web30/custom/buildMyOwn.jsp?agn_id=23264883 and it will be commissionable to Anton Anderssen Travel assuming you type it in exactly. If your name is not on the drop down list, select "Anton Anderssen" as the agent making the booking. Or go to myappleonline.com and type in password apple and user id 23264883. Or call Apple reservations at 800 727 3400 and be sure to tell them to put our Agency Royalty number 232584 into the reservation. Apple Online e-commerce 800 727 3460. Groups 800 315 7871. 800 365 2775 (push option 4 to get the Chicago office) and give them Anton Anderssen Travel's account number 23 264 883 (instead of our true IATA number). If the agency information does not pop up at Apple when you tell them 23 264 883, tell the girl she forgot to type in your name after the number in order to pull up Anton Anderssen agency info. Warning: Do not use that number 23 264 883 for any vendor other than Apple else you will not be getting commission, and the documents will wind up somewhere other than AA Travel. Most of the **specials** can be bought ONLY by **calling** them, as opposed to using the website. At the website, click on "Just for Travel Agents" then in the white box enter user id 23264883. Click on APPLEONLINE 3.0 with password: **apple** (in lower case) Click on RESERVATIONS then GET PRICES. Note: these online prices sometimes are incomplete – you get cheaper prices by phoning in the reservation it seems.

http://www.applevacations.com/servlet/QFD2Web SiteController?PAGEID=1004&OPERATIONID=115&DL VENDORID=0000060264

Groups Dept to Caribbean, Mexico, Hawaii, and Ski resorts.

A.V.-OK Travel protection program includes pre-departure cancellation, tour guard medical program, and price reduction protection.

If you need special assistance, our DSM call 800 365 2776 Sally x2443 Markx2472. 8476401562 fax. Apple Customer Service 800 727 3400. Offer sells charter flights to Cancun, Punta Cana, Puerto Plata, Aruba, Jamaica. Inside sales x2461 John. Travel Agent reduced rates Julie Ann 800 365 2776 x2650 Chicago res ctr 847 640 1170, 847 640 1562 tax Fax to administration 847 640 9761 8476401562   Royalties number 800 365 2776 x5200 Inside Sales 800 365 2776 x2269 Maria or x2461 John

Eleisurelink

http://eleisurelink.com/index.cfm

Ways to book: 1. Send an e-mail to agents@eleisurelink.com. Be sure to include the product ID # (which can be found just below the title on the product page), your date(s) of travel, the number of guests traveling, and any other pertinent information. Please use the name of your agency in the subject box of your e-mail. You will receive a reply within 24-48 hours either confirming, denying, or offering you an alternative to your request.

2. Call (888) 801-8808, press 6, identify which agency you are with and what product you are interested in.

Once you are ready to book your client's vacation, we will need to take payment for the full amount of the trip. Your agency will receive a 10% commission following completion of their travel. All of our vacations are subject to this 10% commission with the exception of our cruises. Those products are purchased at their current selling price and Anton Anderssen Travel Agents are REQUIRED by Anton to add 10% as the commission.

Your Man Tours

http://www.ymtvacations.com/

Your Man Tours, Inc. ,8831 Aviation Blvd., Inglewood, CA 90301   ,1-310-649-3820   1-800-922-9000 vacations@goymt.com

Berkley Tours

http://www.berkleytours.com/

4301 Orchard Lake Road #180, West Bloomfield, Mi 48323. Phone 248 865 8890 or 800 875 8687. Fax 248 865 8928. Motorcoach Tours, Specialized and Customized Group Tours, Theatre Tours, Festival Tours BerkleyTours@aol.com

Cuban Adventures

www.cubanadventures.com

Vancouver, B.C. Canada
Tollfree: 1-877-CUBA FUN (Canada and US) 1-877-282-2386 info@cubanadventures.com

Can Am

Rail/Hotel packages to Chicago, Toronto, Niagara Falls. Phone 248 370 TRIP or 800 347 5566. Fax 248 370 8687

Golf Holidays Int'l

www.golfholidaysintl.com

10815 Rancho Bernardo Rd. Ste 320, San Diego, CA, 92127 toll free (888) 465-3499 res@ghintl.com

ATA LEISURE CORP

- Travel Charter
- ATA Vacations
- American Trans Air

The ATA Leisure vacation travel companies – ATA VACATIONS 800 356 0027, KEY TOURS 800 265 5888,

MAGNA TOURS 800 85 MAGNA and TRAVEL CHARTER 800 521 5267 - are the nation's most reliable and experienced. **Depart from Indy, Chicago, NYC, or Detroit.** Use Anton Anderssen Travel's special IATA number 23 56 1971 to book tours from ATA Leisure. Sales Department fax 248 641 0732.

Travel Charter

http://www.travelcharter.com

Use Anton Anderssen Travel's special IATA number 23 56 1971 to book hotel reservations at Travel Charter / ATA 800 265 5888

- Caribbean Islands
- Costa Rica
- Europe (airfare and rail passes)

Star Tours ☺

http://www.savitours.com/

Phone 800 685 9140 glen@savitours.com startour@jet2.net In Windsor 519 252 8118 Use Anton Anderssen Travel's ARC number 53 40 2591 when making bookings PO Box 32805, Detroit 48232-0805

- Chicago
- Toronto / Niagara Falls

Hillcrest Vacations

http://www.hillcrestvacations.com/

Use Anton Anderssen Travel's ARC number 53 40 2591 when making bookings.. Username Anton password iloveanton 9688 Leslie Street, Unit #10, Richmond Hill, Ontario L4B 4C4, (905) 884-1832 1-800-268-3820

- Montreal
- Vancouver

Happy Tours Vacations

http://www.happytours.com

Phone 831 461 0113, fax 831 461 1604. Toll free: 800 877 4277 (groups ext 9 3024) or groups 800 277 2928; 805 568 1470; or 800 877 3853 x3051. Identify yourself as a travel agent intern for Anton Anderssen Travel, under CLIA number 0056 1971.

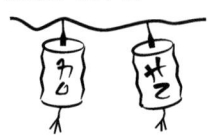

Pacific Delight Tours

http://www.pacificdelighttours.com/
1-800-221-7179 or 212-818-1781. Fax 212-818-1780

Rockwell Tours

http://www.rockwelltours.com/agents/index.asp?site=1971586C056

Use clia number C0561971 or IATA 52431875 Password: iloveanton (800) 526 – 4910 For Caribbean vacations. Call: [1-800-526-4910 x5720] for web problems Fax 954-342-4437 type this url exactly to make the reservations automatically commissionable http://www.rockwelltours.com/agents/index.asp?site=1971586C056

Hotard Vacations

www.neworleanspackages.com
Tel: (800) 984-9003 Fax# (504) 944-8650
Email address: vacations@hotard.com

Travel Impressions

http://www.travimp.com/

Click on the black box at the top right that says "Travel Agent Login" Type in 52431875 for the ARC number (although that's really our IATA number) User ID = Anton, password = lovebug

Gate 1 Travel

http://www.gate1travel.com/agent/

800-682-3333 Click on "Login" on left hand column. Log-in: anton@antontravel.com Password: iloveanton

Inter Island Tours

interislandtours@worldnet.att.net

419 Park Avenue South, NY NY 10016. This tour operator uses American Airlines for the air portion. They offer all the Caribbean and Latin America. Phone 800 245 3434, fax 212 532 4906. Our ID number is 810 757 4177.

Trans Am Tours

http://www.transamtours.com

User Name: antonstudent   Password: iloveant   We specialize in tours to Spain, North America, Central America, and South America, as well as greater Europe in general. 800-822-7600

El Al Israel Tours

Lynn Koppinger, DSM 248 354 3777. Fax 248 354 3944. Reservations 800 223 6700

GoGo Travel

http://www.gogowwv.com

586 228 2500   GOGO Worldwide Vacations   866 332-2220 Ext. 8015 Tell them "Make this commissionable to Anton Anderssen Travel ARC # 53402591 pletcherd@gogowwv.com Need help with an automation booking call 1-800-254-3477

Wildlife Safari Africa

http://www.wildlife-safari.com

African safaris. 800 221 8118 or 925 376 5595. Fax: 925 376 5059. DSM Julie Petschler Julie@wildlife-safari.com

Goway Travel

http://www.goway.com

As a long-haul specialist, Goway is a one-stop shop for travel to AFRICA - air, packages, tours, safaris, groups, etc. Australia & Asia too! Agent must add on at least 10 percent as commission if you are quoted net fares. You are not allowed by Anton Anderssen Travel to book net fares from a supplier then charge the customer only the net fare rate. On our main home page click Travel Agents. You then need to enter: User name antonstudent   Password iloveanton GoWay, 86751 Lincoln Boulevard, Los Angeles, CA 90045 800-387-8850 Fax: 800-665-4432 Email: res@goway.com Jerry Horn jhorn1@attglobal.net fax 310 410 3972 Booking site: http://www.goway.com/cgi-bin/protect/mojoProtector.cgi?type=member

username: anton   password: iloveanton

Four Seasons Hotels

http://www.fshr.com

As the world's leading operator of luxury hotels and resorts, Four Seasons currently manages 51 properties in 23 countries, primarily under the Four Seasons and Regent brands. Call 1 800 819-5053 Use CLIA 00 56 1971

Outrigger Hotels

http://www.outrigger.com
1 800 OUTRIGGER

- Hawaii
- South Pacific
- Australia

800 688 7444 Outrigger offers the very best value for hotels in Hawaii! Their family / budget properties are called Ohana Hotels. They own the largest number of properties in Waikiki and are clean, comfortable, and close to the important attractions. Use CLIA number 00 56 1971 when they ask for a number. If you have any clients staying at this chain, be sure to fill out the Outrigger Specialist Amenity form so your customer get a free gift. www.outrigger.com/specialist

Marc Resorts Hawaii

www.marcresorts.com/travelagents/login.asp

Click on the reservations link at the bottom of the website. Use email Anton@AntonTravel.com Password (case sensitive): vAQd72Fs IATA: 53402591 If you experience any problems, please call 1-800-535-0085. Toll-Free Reservations 1-800-535-0085 • fax: 1-800-633-5085

Aston Hotels Hawaii

http://www.aston-hotels.com

800 922 7866 or (877) 997-6667 Aston hotels offers a large variety of properties in Hawaii. From Shabby to Chic.

DER Europe Travel ☺

http://www.dertravel.com/travelAgents/

9501 West Devon Ave

Rosemont, IL 60018

888-337-7350 Phone

847-430-0000 Phone

800-282-7474 Fax

847-692-4165 Fax

Use Anton Anderssen Travel's account number 95 23 4177 when booking vacations with DER. Click on the words "Travel Agent" in the left hand column of the web site. You must use Internet Explorer (not netscape) for full web site utilization.

DER offers every travel component, from international flights and hotels to transportation components like rail and car rentals. They offer both independent and escorted tours to the most popular destinations in Europe as well as exciting group programs worldwide. DER backs all of its programs with the USTOA $1 million protection plan, decades of experience and proven reliability. DER uses over 30 scheduled airlines to over 300 destinations worldwide! They offer open-jaw and one-way flights, some European and South Pacific originations, and free $100,000 flight insurance. Advance seat assignments and frequent flyer mileage accrual is available through many airlines.

Disney Travel Company

www.disneytravelagents.com

disneyworld.com

(800) 327-2996 travel agents only, (407) 828 8101 (res for general public) Use Anton Anderssen Travel's CLIA number 00 56 1971 or IATA number 52431875. Make sure you tell them to make it commissionable. If they try to tell you that reservations made thru "Central Reservations" is non-commissionable speak to a supervisor or ask for Ace (he's very competent) Inside Sales Fax 407-3450137 or 407-566-6151. Travel Agency Sales Office (order brochures) 800 939 8265 407 566 6136. Tim Jones is sales rep for Detroit. To get brochures in French fax a request to Janis at 416 923 9765. Sales Support fax 407 345 0137

The Orlando MagicCard is available free of charge, by calling 1-800-643-9492. It offers a variety of rental car, off-site hotel, and entertainment, shopping and dining discounts in the Orlando area.

Free video or DVD about a vacation in Disney World call 800 965 8989. Call and get one if you know anyone wanting to go to Disney this year. For free Disney Cruise Line video call 888 DCL 8181.

Universal Parks & Resorts

www.universaltravelagents.com

Username antonstudent password: iloveanton Will issue you passwords after you have 3 tour bookings completed.

Hotel & Travel Index

http://www.htihotelink.com/

Over 78,000 Hotels... For Travel Professionals. Includes fams.

Hotel Guide

http://www.hotelguide.com/affiliate/5580_1.cfm?lang=en - English
http://www.hotelguide.com/affiliate/5580_1.cfm?lang=en &searchtype=extendedsearch

65,000 Hotels around the world and their descriptions.

Rail Europe

www.raileurope.com

Eurail Passes. 800 4 Eurail. Our DSM is Tim Galloway phone 763 422 8226, fax 763 422 8227.

British Holidays

www.BAHolidays.com

877 428 2228 British Holidays is a sister company to British Airways, so it uses BA for its flights and makes the airfare portion commissionable. Use our ARC number. To reconfirm flights call 800 247 9297

Mayflower Tours

www.mayflowertours.com

Deluxe escorted tours worldwide. 1225 Warren Ave Downers Grove, IL 60515 Phone:(800)323-7604 or 630 874 5501 Fax:(630)960-3575 Mary Toth or sherri@mayflowertours.com

Ya'lla Tours

www.yallatours.com

Ya'lla Tours USA 4711 SW Huber St., suite # 1 Portland, OR 97219 Tel: (503) 977-3758, 800-644-1595 ext. 101 Fax: (503) 977-3765

European Tours

www.europtours.com

Greece, Italy, Turkey, France, Spain, Britain. Call 800 882 3983. Fax 213 624 4898

Consolidator Shopper

http://www.consolidatorshopper.com

LoginID: antonstudent Password: iloveanton When the screen first shows you have to select the area of the world you want. Click on Power Search. You must add at least 10% to fares as a commission. If you fail to add at least 10% to ANY NET fare for any supplier for any passenger, you automatically authorize Anton to cancel your reservation, even if it is non refundable and non changeable. Using Anton's accounts means you expressly agree to adding a commission to any NET fare, else you risk forfeiting your entire amount paid for any fare, and there is NO recourse for you. Don't try to be clever and try to get around adding the commission to NET fares. Anton will see the reports and cancel your reservations if you try to skirt the commission.

When using Consolidator Shopper, there are frequently differences between cash and credit card pricing. This depends on the airline and the individual consolidator company. It all shakes out when you get to the final pricing step.

This and refund/change charges are two of the things you have to research if you have multiple consolidator companies on the same route and you can do so before finalizing any purchase. I print out the fare rules and compare the side by side to check. I also price them out up to the point of purchase.

Cash or credit final price will not affect your fee at all -- unless you've quoted a price to the client and now find it's higher because of payment by credit card. I would always to quote and recommend payment by credit card.

What are consolidators and why should I use one?

An airline consolidator is a company that has various volume based airfare agreements with one or more airlines. Due to the consolidators productivity and relationships with its carriers, it is able offer to you, the Travel Agent, an opportunity to provide a discount to your retail customer, while at the same time, freeing you from the limited income you are subjected to in issuing International tickets due to commission caps.

One of the most important reasons to utilize consolidator tickets is that you can control the amount of money you are able to make on a ticket. Sky Bird Travel provides you with net airfares allowing you to determine your own commission by adding a markup of your own choosing. You can decide how competitive you wish that fare to be. Also, you will add any applicable taxes, government fees or surcharges to that fare for the customer to pay. At the end of the day, you have the opportunity to earn more than you normally would by issuing a ticket through your normal Computer Reservations System (CRS) procedure.

Sky Bird sells seats from airline inventory at discounted contract prices. We have over 7,000,000 fares available on our web site. A flight's inventory can have numerous airfare discount levels depending on the route and competitive market conditions. These price levels are subject to change by the various carriers depending on a variety of conditions they feel are necessary to review in determining the flight or route's profitability. Thus, these fares may rise and fall a number of times and may change at the carrier's discretion, sometimes daily. Therefore, an airfare is only guaranteed after the ticket is purchased.

For certain Business Class or published discount fares that may at times be as low as or lower than some of our consolidator rates, Sky Bird can often issue those tickets on your behalf, but with the advantage that you can still receive a higher commission level than if you had issued it yourself.

Also, Sky Bird Travel does not sell directly to the consumer. We will not compete with you in the marketplace. Our fares can be accessed only through the 4 major CRS or through our web site, which requires an ARC, IATA or CLIA number in order to receive a password for accessing fares. You are our partners, not our competitors.

As you read through the information in our web site, you will find that there are numerous reasons why you should be using a consolidator for all of your international travel.

Sky Bird

http://www.SkyBird-Travel.com

This is a consolidator based in Southfield Michigan. Net rates do not have the commission, therefore you are required to add at least 10% commission to the net fare for ALL passengers, including yourself. Using Anton's licenses means you agree to this requirement. 248 372 4800 or 888 SKY BIRD.   UserID anton password iloveanton   Inquiries x218 Monique

C & H Int'l

http://www.cnhintl.com/

User id: anton Password: iloveanton 27777 Franklin Rd. Suite 125 Southfield, MI 48034   (248) 784-5304 or (248) 784-5305 . Fax   (248) 784-5306   Also: 29 E Madison, Suite 1309,
Chicago, IL 60602 (312) 782-2288 or
(888) 303-2288. Fax (312) 346-8785

Greaves Travel

http://www.greaves-travel.com

Chicago 312 279 7333. Consolidator for British Airways.

Cosmopolitan Travel

http://www.ctsfares.com/

Login   :AntonStudent   Password : iloveanton Cosmopolitan sells net (non commissionable, therefore add 10% to net price) and commissionable trans-atlantic international airfares. Specialists to Greece. 22313 Mack Av, St Clair Shore Mi 48080. Phone 586 445 8585 Ask for Brom. 800 633 4087. Fax 586 445 6194 Brom at home 248 357 1813 or cell 248 854 6107

Apollo Consolidator

www.ApolloFares.com

1-800-500-8415 / (312) 236-7356 x3 Fax: (312) 236-7404 307 North Michigan Ave. Suite 200   Chicago, IL. 60601   Gives commission on British Airways and other overseas flights. If you are booking a NET fare, Anton requires you to add at least 10 percent as commission. Login: antonstudent Password: iloveanton

Unitravel Consolidator

www.unitravel.com

800-325-2222 Use Anton Anderssen Travel phone 586 757 4177 as the account number when making bookings. Add 10% commission to net fares (required) for non-commissionable tickets

Europe Rail

www.eurogroups.com

Eurailpass, European country rail tickets, hotels, custom tours. 800 462 2577 Use CLIA 00 56 1971.

Kemwel Holiday Autos

www.kemwel.com

Deep discount car rental rates world wide. Phone: 800 678 0678 or 800-576-1590. Fax: 207 842 2223. Use IATA number 52431875 Your clients can enjoy the same internet booking discount currently offered on kha's public web site, by simply placing code tad01 in the special code field in the booking engine.

Dollar Rent a Car

http://www.dollar.com

Click on the "Travel Agents" button and enter Anton Anderssen Travel's special IATA number 00 56 1971. Telephone 800 800 4000 (Ask for promo code Globe (Florida only) or New or Trib

Thrifty Rent a Car

http://www.thrifty.com/TravelAgent/

800 367 2277   1-800-527-7075 Click on the "Travel Agents" button. Reservations: 800 THRIFTY. Sign up for gold points on line. Sign up for Blue Chip Express free or call 888 400 8877. Corp accounts 800 331 3550. You can use your Wal-Mart credit card.

National Car Rental

http://www.NationalCar.com

Reservations 800 Car Rent. Commercial Accounts 800 328 8018 option 3. Keith x8622.

Alamo Rent a Car ☺

http://www.ta.alamo.com

Call 800 4 Agents ext 2.   Use IATA License 52 43 1875 (or if that doesn't work then Alamo account number 801279) to identify yourself as Anton Anderssen Travel. Tell them your traveler has a discount with Alamo and you are requesting rate code BY and ID: 687743. Also tell them you have an "Alamo Cash In Club number 52477" Agent "Cash In Club" 800 984 9492 Commission dept. Rate code TA 6775 for agents

Avis Rent a Car

http://www.avisagent.com

Call Avis at 800 331 1212 and supply Anton Anderssen Travel's CLIA account number 00 56 1971 to identify yourself as an agent with Anton Anderssen travel. Tell Avis your Club Red number is 198450. Tell Avis your customer has an Avis Worldwide Discount number L672984 and that your customer is a member of Perks at Work discount program.

Budget Rent a Car

http://www.budget.com

800 527 0700 If calling in the reservation tell the reservations agent to put Pin zd000004201 in the ZD field. Tell them your customer has a discount ID: BCD-X518600 When booking via internet, click on "Travel Agents Only" at the top right; enter IATA number 52431875 and unlimited budget number zd000004201. Rate code U030025 will give special discounts on trucks. Commission problems? 800 435 7100 option 2 or Fax 877 363 8691.

Hertz Car Rental

http://hertzagent.com/
https://www.hertz.com/business_09/agencies/index.html

At the web site, click on "Travel Agents" Use IATA number 52 43 1875. Use "Exactly Rewards" ID ER746777 For Reservations in the U.S.A. call 800-654-3131. For International Reservations call 800-654-3001. Hertz Corporate Discount # 69212 and Rate Code GTKY to get "travel agent only" rates https://www2.hertz.com/travelagent/agentup/index.cfm

Cruise Lines Brochures

www.cruise4.com/CruiseBrochures.html

7 World's Leading Cruises

http://www.worldsleadingcruiselines.com/agents/home.asp

From the seven World's Leading Cruise Lines, a NEW and EXCLUSIVE site to assist our valued travel partners ...accelerate their e-marketing and cruise sales! Click on a cruise logo to learn more about their features, amenities, and destinations.   User id is Anton@AntonTravel.com and password is iloveanton

Carnival Cruise Lines ☺

http://www.bookccl.com/

http://content.onlineagency.com/sites/5134/index.asp?site=5134&tide=5074

http://cruises.aregood.com

Glitz and glitter, like a floating Las Vegas. When calling in a booking, use Anton Anderssen Travel's telephone number 586 757 4177, and CLIA number 00 56 1971. Phone Carnival 800 327 9501 (individuals) or 800 327 5782 / 305 599 2666 (groups). If using the internet, go to www.bookccl.com, click on LOGIN and enter ID: student and password: iloveanton   After you log on, you can see all the specials which have been faxed to us at http://www.bookccl.com/salestools/FunFaxes/default.asp   Carnival is the world's most popular cruise line. To get brochures, click on the brochures button but use your address in the boxes instead of Anton Anderssen Travel, so it comes to your house. For brochures, you can call Carnival's Inside Sales Team at (800) 327-7276. Carnival fun ship website support desk 800 845 2599 from 9am to

8pm. To get brochures, just go to http://www.bookccl.com/ click on LOGIN, LoginID= student password= iloveanton At the scroll down bar which says Sales and Collateral scroll down to Brochure Request. Select 50 Fleet brochures, then click Continue. Type over the info for the address part only. Revenue Accounting 9:00AM - 5:30PM (Mon - Fri) 800 327 7276 FL/Nat/CN 305-599-2600. Inside Sales 800 327 7276. Special Events / Agent reduced rates 888 901 7787. Research department fax 305 406 5882

Holland America Cruises

http://hal.com/

Holland America Cruises (kind of like a floating country club) they are adding a lot off spa amenities. The IATA id on file with HAL is 5243187 (the last digit is left off of the IATA number in their computer) 800-426-0327 Groups x4039 Brochures call toll-free 1-800-626-9900. 800 663 5384 Canadian brochures. Internet help desk 800-207-3545. Operations Support Desk fax 206 281 0619 www.hollandamerica.com/TAHQtemplate.jsp Website ID: AntonStudent password: iloveanton Sales Rep Barbara Wright (800-544-0443, ext. 4834)   Holland America Academy hollandamerica.com , go into travel agent headquarters, click on link on left side. Free Training course. www.halpromos.com for specials.   HAL Alaska fams 206 301 5290

Costa Cruises 800-462-6782 or 800 Go Costa. Reservations, 800-327-2537 Sales. Collateral 800 33 Costa. Faxback 877 FYI Costa

Seabourn Cruises 800-929-9595

Windstar Sail Cruises 800-258-SAIL

Cunard Line 800-528-6273, 800 5 Cunard http://www.cunard.com/flextools/ login: anton password: iloveanton

Vacations on Video (ship videos) 800-323-4617

Disney Cruise Lines

Use Anton Anderssen Travel's number 586 757 4177. Phone Disney Cruise Lines at 800 511 1333 or (800) 951-3532. DSM 800 939 9265 (sales dept.) (877) 566-0972 http://dcl.reservations.disney.go.com/cgi-bin/WebObjects/TravelCL.woa/wa/TravelAgentLogin type in Agency Phone 5867574177 affiliation number 00561971 type of affiliation: CLIA

Norwegian Cruise Lines ☺

http://www.bookncl.com

http://www.ncl.com

Use Anton Anderssen Travel's number 586 757 4177, and CLIA number 00 56 1971. Phone NCL at 800 327 7030 x1 x1. For Hawaii sailings call 1-888-NCL-HAWAII For promotions, call 800 FAX NCL1 and leave your fax number. Carolyn Pugh is our DSM 313 387 8920 Sales Office Fax (631) 514-3006. The travel partners section at www.ncl.com has lots of info: User Name : sell Password : norwegian (only valid at www.ncl.com, not www.bookncl.com). For www.bookncl.com use ID student and password iloveanton. Ready-made flyers are available to distribute at http://www.ncl.com/dailydeals/index.htm NCL Passenger Courtesy Department x1106 Re-accommodations 800 625 4309 Our sales rep is Carolyn Pugh 313 387 8920

Orient Cruise Lines

http://www.orientlines.com

Use Anton Anderssen Travel's number 586 757 4177, and CLIA number 00 56 1971. Phone Orient at 800 333 7300   Our sales rep is Carolyn Pugh 313 387 8920

Royal Caribbean ☺

http://content.onlineagency.com/cache_html/182 02_5135.htm

www.CruisingPower.com

General Cruise Reservations 800 327 6700
Inside Sales: 800 327 2056 fax 800 722 5329
Group 800 722 5476   Use Anton Anderssen Travel's number 586 757 4177, and CLIA number 00 56 1971. Our DSM is Verlonda Curry 248 355 3930 vcurry@rccl.com . Commission problems 305 539 5337 CruisingPower.com User ID: 217586139 Password: iloveanton Web/Automation support desk 800-443-5789. RCCL Brochures 800 255 4373 800 255 4373. Celebrity brochures 800 211 4789.

Radisson 7 Seas Cruises

http://www.rssc.com/enews.html

Use Anton Anderssen Travel's number 586 757 4177, and CLIA number 00 56 1971. Reservations: Toll-Free (866) 217-1374

Group Reservations: (800) 914-5500

Sales Service: (800) 477-7500, ext. 600

email to rsscresv@radisson.com.

Princess Cruise Lines

http://www.princess.com/agent/

Princess is also known as "The Love Boat" on TV. Click on "Travel Agent Center" Use Anton Anderssen Travel's telephone number 586 757 4177, and CLIA number 00 56 1971. Go to the website and click on "Travel Agent booking system" User ID AntonStudent password iloveanton Call 800 421 1700. Sales office Julie Grace

877 888 1869 x44866   Sales office fax 661 284 4745. 800 545 0008 Jill Domino extension 44880 in Customer Service. 661 284 4880 direct line to Jill.

Crystal Cruise Lines

http://agent.crystalcruises.com

Condé Nast Traveler readers have again voted Crystal Cruises the "Best Large-Ship Cruise Line" for a record seventh consecutive year. For Reservations in the US and Canada call (800) 446-6620. Inside sales x6 DSM Tim Rinkoski

Seabourn Cruise Lines

http://seabourn.com

For Reservations in the US and Canada call (800) 929 9595.

World Explorer Cruises

http://www.wecruise.com

Voyages of discovery, learning and adventure. Reservations 800 854 3835 , Brochures 800 325 2752, Fax 415 820 9292

Viking River Cruises

http://www.vikingrivercruises.com

Call 877 668 4546. Tell them to give you 14% commission because we belong to THOR consortium. River cruising in Europe, Russia, and China.

eWaterways

http://www.bvassociates.net/online/affiliate.asp?AffId=470&Logo=1

Canal Barges & River Boat Cruises Tel: (800) 546-4777 Fx: (212) 688-9467

B&V Apartments Europe

*http://www.bvassociates.net/online/affiliate.asp?
AffId=470&Logo=2*

Over 15,000 appartment units in Europe. Phone: 800 755-8266 or +1 212 688-9489; Fax: +1 212 688-9467

River Barge USA

*http://www.bvassociates.net/online/affiliate.asp?
AffId=470&Logo=5*

Tel: (800) 546-4777 Fx: (212) 688-9467

America West Vacations ☺

awvtravelagents.com

Not to be confused with America West Airlines. This is a sister company that uses America West unpublished bulk air plus some type of land package like car or hotel nights. You can't buy just airfare. Call 1-800-356-6611 or 877 211 9762 Use Anton Anderssen Travel's Acct # 00 56 1971. When booking online, click the purple button "Book Your Vacation" on the far left underneath the word Travel Agents, then on the next screen where it asks for IATA or CLIA number type in CL561971. Internet help desk assistance (800) 442-5013 Las Vegas * Arizona * Mexico * California * Across America.

GTS GloboTours

http://www.globotours.net/home.asp

18725 East Gale Ave. Suite # 209 City Of Industry, CA 91748 Tel: (800) 988-4833 Fax: (626) 839-8613. Use number 810 757 4177.

Globus / Cosmos Tours

http://www.globusandcosmos.com/

Call 800 221 0090 Use Anton Anderssen Travel's number 810 757 4177. Know the tour code (a four digit number) and departure number (references when the land tour starts) from the brochures.

Branson Vacation Tours

http://www.bransonvacationtours.com/

Call 800 417 6122 Use Anton Anderssen Travel's CLIA # 00 56 1971

Trafalgar Tours

http://www.TrafalgarTours.com/

Call 800 800 854 0103 Use Anton Anderssen Travel's CLIA # 00 56 1971. For display materials fax your request to 313 274 9636. Our DSM is Julie Petschler 800 626 6604 ext 3274. Brochures: 1.800.352.4444 Reservations: 800-854-0103 Groups: 800-626-6603 Book Online: www.booktt.com Order Brochures: www.trafalgarbrochures.com

SMI Ireland Tours

http://www.SMIreland.com/

Call 800 449 1899. Our DSM is Rose Weiler.

Travel Guard Travel Insurance ☺

http://www.travelguard.com/

Brian Hoch. 1145 Clark St., Stevens Point, WI 54481 Tel: 715-345-1041 ext 1514, or 800-826-7791 ext 1514, 800-826-0838 fax, email: bhoch@travelguard.com customer service at 800-826-1300 Local rep: Chris Dritlein, cdritlein@noelgroup.com 248 528 9229 phone, 248 528 1703 fax. Listed under ARC number **53 40 2591** Be sure to click on the "AgentLink" button at the top right corner to get commissions. The blue page should turn orange and say "Anton Anderssen Travel" on the page as your confirmation you are making a commissionable booking.

Travel Insured Insurance

http:// www.travelinsured.com

Teresa Giacalone Regional Sales Manager Travel Insured International (800) 243-3174, x129 Fax: (860) 528-7663 tgiacalone@travelinsured.com

Travelex Travel Insurance

http://travelex-insurance.com

For all kinds of travel insurance. 800 537 8052 800 877 1039. Fax 888 369 8481. Eric Anderson is our DSM.

Student Express

http:// www.studentexpress.com

Click on the button at the top that says Travel Agent Login. Sean Weed is the sales Director. 800 444 2373 x109 or 303 696 1155 (Denver CO) Fax 303 696 1166 email sweed@studentexpress.com For internet problems call 1-800-787-3787. Dan in Colorado x114 sales mgr.

Student Break Tours

http://www.studentbreaks.com/

135 E Grand River Av, E Lansing Mich 48823. Tel: 800 S Break 1.   They have charters to Cancun, and work only with the Oasis Cancun hotel.

Endless Summer Tours

http://www.endlesssummertours.com/
Student Spring Break Tours. 800 234 7007

Student Travel Services

http://www.ststravel.com
Student Travel Services 1413 Madison Park Drive Glen Burnie, MD 21061 Tel. 1.800.648.4849
Fax. 1.410.787.9580 Click on Agent Login. User name: 52431875 password iloveanton

Hawaii Activities

www.hawaiiactivities.com/index.cfm?ta=signin
Any time you wish to make reservations for your clients, simply enter your login – anton@antontravel.com - on our Travel Agents page. (Click the Travel Agents Button) You MUST login before making any reservations so that we can properly track your sales and get an accurate commission check to your agency every quarter!   1-877-877-1222

Sports Tours

http://www.esotericsportstours.com/

Esoteric Sports Tours 2005 Woods River Lane Duluth, GA 30097 Phone: 800-321-8008 Fax: 770-622-8866 info@esotericsportstours.com Business Hours: Monday – Friday 9:00 am - 6:00 pm EST

All About Tours

http://www.allabouthawaii.com
http://www.allabouthawaii.com/index.phtml?ARC=53402591

800-274-8687 888-592-5077 Hawaii, Reno, Las Vegas, and California. Email them at hawaii@allabouthawaii.com Use our IATA number 52431875 and security code HKI4G96Q (that's a capital "i" after the letter k) when booking online, or just use link http://www.allabouthawaii.com/index.phtml?ARC=52431875 and it will make it commissionable automatically Fax 800 233 0663

Blue Sky Tours ☺

http://www.BlueSkyTours.com/

Blue Sky phone 800 678 2787 or fax 800 747 1221 Supply Anton Anderssen Travel's Acct # 23 757 417(7). Internet logon ID anton@antontravel.com password love4anton Hawaii tours. Deirdre is sales marketing rep ext. 2203 They pay commission on published airfares to Hawaii too. Flyers Charlotte Kerr (in house sales rep, makes flyers) 800 678 2787 x 2157

FunJet ☺

http://www.AntonFunJet.com/ ☺
http://www.FunJetAgent.com/

You can go to www.AntonFunjet.com and it will automatically make sales commissionable to Anton Anderssen Travel without having to know the passwords, but make sure you see the words "Anton Anderssen Travel" at the top of the screen. Or go to Funjet Agency Advantage www.FunJetAgent.com. Account = 8107574177 User Name = Anton Student Password = (ask Anton for it after you've booked several Funjet by phone) FunJet 800 669 4466 x1 reservations, 800 558 3050 Funjet Agency Services ext 6913 fax 414 351 5844 Funjet Hawaii 888 310 8965 Funjet Customer Service 800 558 3060 Our sales rep is Beth Ann Kirk 800 558 3060 x 1606. Travel Agent reduced rate fax 414 932 2132 attn: Opal. Travel Agent reduced rate supervisor Tkriese@MarkTravel.com

WHAT IS CHARTER AIR? SCHEDULED AIR?

Charter Airfare

Funjet Vacations isn't an airline and we don't own any planes. We contract with charter airlines for the use of their aircraft to various destinations. We provide the passengers and the airline provides everything else that goes with your flight. Because we contract in large volumes, we are able to pass significant savings on to you. The difference between a "scheduled" flight and a charter flight is that charter flights are scheduled on certain days each week and may not depart every day as scheduled airlines do. An example of a charter pattern is Thursday/Sunday, which departs Thursday and comes home Sunday. The same passengers go and return together on the same aircraft and everyone on the plane is on vacation.

For lower fares, nonstop flights and great value, Funjet Vacations offers charter flights with ATA Airlines, Champion Air, Ryan Air, Trans Meridian Airlines, Midwest Airlines, and Southwest Airlines. Each of these airlines has a superior reputation for safety, reliability and friendly service, complemented with fleets that are among the most reliable and most well maintained in the industry. The charter airlines we deal with use various types of aircraft ranging from 727's to 757's which seats approximately 247 passengers.

New Planes! Not Your Typical Charter Airplanes

Many of our partners have newer state-of-the-art, more fuel efficient fleet which allows us to lower our fuel costs and pass the savings on to you. On average, these Boeing 737-800, A320 and A321 planes are 2 years old with a seat pitch of 31", which means more legroom and more comfort when you are traveling. Wide, comfortable seats are arranged three across on both sides of the aisle on these aircraft, and coupled with our unparalleled service, you will enjoy a fun-filled vacation!

Mark Travel Corporation

http://www.marktravel.com/

AeroMexico Vacations, Adventure Tours, Funjet Vacations (Formerly known as Hamilton Miller Hudson Fayne), MexSeaSun Vacations, MGM Mirage Vacations, Mountain Vacations, Town and Country Tours, Transglobal Vacations, Southwest Airlines Vacations 800 423 5683, Vacations by Sun Country, United Vacations and US Airways Vacations. When they ask for the IATA number give them Anton Anderssen Travel number 810 757 4177 instead.

Continental Air Vacations

http://www.covacations.com/agents.aspx

Not to be confused with Continental Airlines. A sister company of Continental Airlines, uses Continental for unpublished bulk air and has land packages all over the world. You cannot book just air. It must be air plus something else like car or hotel nights. Call 800 301 3800. Sales Support When they ask for the IATA number give them 810 757 4177. UserID: Anton Student password: iloveanton Web site help desk 1-888-346-3651. At the web site, go to the very bottom of the screen and click on Travel Agents.

Delta Dream Vacations

http://www.DeltaVacations.com/

Not to be confused with Delta Airlines. A totally different company from Delta Airlines, uses Delta for unpublished bulk air and has land packages all over the world. You cannot book just air. It must be air plus something else like car or hotel nights. Call 800 221 6666 (we like to work with Betsy at x5181) ; or 888 714 4435. When they ask for the IATA number give them the Anton Anderssen Travel's account # 810 757 4177 instead! On website click on "travel agents" in the blue box at the left. They use a pseudo IATA 8107574177 user name = Anton Student, and password = iloveanton

Future Vacations

http://www.futurevacations.com/

At the very bottom of the web page click on Travel Agents. User ID and password is same as VAX. This is a sister company of Delta Dream Vacations. Book via VAX for 14% commission (you must manually increase the commission amount). For a lower commission rate, phone them at 800 456 2323. For group travel call 800 301 3300.

Pleasant Holidays

PleasantAgent.com

http://www.pleasant.net

Pleasant Holidays phone 1-800-7HAWAII , 800 2 Hawaii, 800 442 3234, or 800 448 3330 (Mexico). 1-800-742-9244 Use Anton Anderssen Travel's Acct # 58656 for Hawaii or Mexico, or Acct # 58517 for South Pacific and Orient.   Fax 619 283 3131.   Air Only 800 877 8111. Sales Department 800-442-3234. At the web site click on the "Travel Agents Only" link. User ID: antonstudent password iloveanton agent id number 58656 Pleasant's Internet Support desk: net-support@pleasant.net or call 1-800-482-2865. Sales department 800 442 3234. Linda Morton is our sales rep.

- Hawaii 800 2 Hawaii
- Tahiti, Fiji 888 636 2001
- Mexico and Caribbean 800 448 3333
- Australia, NZ 888 636 2001
- Tahiti Fiji 888 636 2001
- Asia 800 377 1080

Custom Vacations

http://www.classiccustomvacations.com/classic/pdf/forms/fax_booking_form.pdf

http://www.classiccustomvacations.com/classic/hawaii/teaser/2001-preview.htm

Classic Custom Vacations 800 221 3949. They list our CLIA license 00561971 in their database to identify our

agency. Use 00561971 whenever they ask for the IATA number (even though it's not really our IATA number)
- Hawaii
- Caribbean
- Europe
- Mexico
- US

Classic Custom Vacations is a partner with ExpediaForAgents.com 00561971 Nora Berna is our DSM

DFW Tours

http://www.dfwtours.com/

Dallas Fort Work. 800 527 2589 ID: student password: iloveanton When fares are quoted as NET you are REQUIRED to add 10% as a travel agency commission

Airline contact phone numbers for your convenience:
American Airlines: 1-800-433-7300
America West Airlines: 1-800-235-9292
Continental Airlines: 1-800-525-0280
Delta Airlines: 1-800-221-1212
Northwest Airlines: 1-800-225-2525
Southwest Airlines: 1-800-435-9792 or 800 428 4377
TWA: 1-800-221-2000
United Airlines: 1-800-241-6522
Air Canada: 1-888-247-2262
Air France: 1-800-237-2747
British Airways: 1-800-247-9297
KLM: 1-800-438-5000
Lufthansa: 1-800-645-3880
Virgin Atlantic: 1-800-862-8621

Remember you will NEVER get commission from these airlines DIRECTLY even if you completely create the airline ticket by yourself totally from start to finish by booking from a GDS CRS and totally writing every aspect of the airline ticket yourself. If you call an airline directly to make a booking they don't pay commission because they feel if they are the ones doing the work creating the booking then they keep all commissions. That's why we use tour operators. Tour operators are happy to write airline tickets for us and we still get commission. Don't confuse companies like Delta Airlines (an airline) with Delta Airlines Vacations (a tour operator). Delta Airlines will NOT give you a commission, but Delta Airlines VACATIONS does pay a commission to travel agencies.

Qwik Park Detroit

http://www.qwikpark.com/

Our preferred supplier for parking at the airport in Detroit is Qwik Park. Download coupons from the internet and make sure where it says "courtesy of" that you write Anton Anderssen Travel on it.

NW Airlines

Scheduled airlines usually don't pay commission to travel agencies any more. If you buy a ticket DIRECTLY from NW, you don't get commission plus they expect you to do all the work. Instead, use a tour operator listed in this handout which uses their own charter airplanes or bulk seats on national carriers, but you get commission because you're NOT buying directly from the airline. Spirit DOES pay commissions.

New York City Vacations

http://www.nycvp.com/

- A full range of mid-town Manhattan hotels
- Sightseeing throughout the City
- Rail fare on Amtrak throughout the Northeast corridor
- Discounted airfare on US Airways and United Airlines
- Broadway Theatre "Best Seats in the House"

Call 888 692 8701. Use Anton Anderssen Travel's old phone number 810 757 4177, and CLIA number 00 56 1971.

Theatre Direct Tickets

http://www.broadway.com/affiliate/travel_agent.asp

- New York Theatre news
- Specials for Groups

Use Anton Anderssen Travel's ARC number 5340259 (actually the last digit is dropped) 1650 Broadway #910 * NY, NY 10019 Phone 1-800-BROADWAY / 212-541-8457 * Fax 212-541-4892

Vacation Land

http://www.vacation-land.com/

Call 800 245 0050. Packages to Hong Kong

Amtrak Vacations

http://www.AmTrak.com/

Call 800 321 8684. Use Anton Anderssen Travel's Phone number 810 757 4177. When they ask for an IATA number tell them 00 56 1971 (even though really this is our CLIA number)

Universal Studio Vacations

www.universaltravelagents.com

universalstudiosvacations.com

Call 800 224 3838. When they ask for an IATA number tell them 00 56 1971 (even though really this is our CLIA number) They will book flights, hotels, theme park tickets, and more. For brochures and collateral, call 407

363 8000, 800 550 1849. Travel Industry Sales Department 877 U Escape (407) 363 8624, fax (407) 224 6424. For free video call 407 363 8000 x7 After you earned your ID card and passed the specialist exams call 407-224-6448 to book your special Travel Agent Package.

Shore Trips

http://www.shoretrips.com/agents/linkhome.asp?linkid=st1540

User ID 5243187 (this is the first seven digits of our IATA number) Password IloveAnton They represent 400 tour operators on 22 Caribbean Islands who bring you over 1000 ShoreTrips®!"

Soaring Eagle Resort

Mt Pleasant Michigan 877 232 4532, 989 775 5777. Use IATA 52431875

Ski Vacation Planners

www.skivacationplanners.com
800 822-6754

Destinations Ireland and England

Call 800 832 1848. Fax 212 741 1050. Golf Tours, Castles & Manors, Honeymoons.

Atlantis Events

http://www.atlantisevents.com

Call 800-628-5268 800-6-ATLANTIS Fax: 310-281-5455
Atlantis is the largest gay and lesbian tour company in the world, offering a wide range of cruise, resort, and tour packages. We work with name brand companies to deliver the highest quality and best value vacations available today to the gay and lesbian traveler. As an Atlantis Agent, you will certainly provide your clients with the best gay vacation experience available.

Frequently Asked Questions

Since I am a travel agent student am I going to get everything for free from now on? No. Usually the only way to get travel free is to be the tour conductor in a group.

How can I get faxes or emails about the bargains the suppliers are advertising? For emails, sign up at http://groups.yahoo.com/group/antontravel

Why would I want to be a travel agent for Anton Anderssen Travel? So you don't have to pay $5,000.00 for tuition at a travel school to learn stuff you'll never use! If you're going to travel, you may as well get travel agent credit for products you book for your own use!

Will I get paid while working as an intern? Yes! You will receive 50% of all commission received by Anton Anderssen Travel, plus free education, plus the perks that are awarded to **productive** travel agents. You **earn** the perks.

Can my friends be travel agents? If you personally write to Anton at Anton@AntonTravel.com and recommend them then yes. Otherwise, you must be known to Anton.

Can I book travel products from any supplier? If it's a cruise line, yes, you can book as an Anton Anderssen Travel Agent with any cruise line. Otherwise, not until you talk to Anton and he screens the supplier as safe. It's a better idea to stick to a few good suppliers. Anton Anderssen travel wants to make sure you are educated on a select number of vendors rather than trying to know them all. Always sell travel insurance to the passengers unless they refuse it!

How do I get my documents? You will need to get them from Anton Anderssen Travel. 4177 Garrick Av, Warren Mi 48091 or they can be mailed to your house. Telephone 586 757 4177 after 12 noon.

How can I receive faxes? Sign up for free fax services www.efax.com/free (if you only type in www.efax.com you will have to pay for the service so pay attention to what you type ☺) To read the efaxes that Anton sends you, download the free efax reader software at www.efax.com/need

What will Anton Anderssen Travel do with the money it receives in commissions from the suppliers I book travel with? Pay off the $25,000 ARC bond required to be a licensed agency.

What if the customer makes changes which results in fees? The supplier must bill the customer's charge card, not take the fee out of the commission payable to the Agency. You must make sure all clients are billed for the vacation price, not having the supplier remove funds from the commission to pay for part of the customer's vacation. If you fail to do so, it comes out of your share of the commission and you will be asked to find a new host agency.

Can I have a travel agent discount when I book trips from suppliers for myself? Anton will specifically tell you the perks you can have as an intern. As a rule of thumb, you can have perks, but you can't have discounts. A perk is something like a Seminar or Educational Study Tour for travel agents only. If you are booking something that is sold to the general public, you must pay the "commissionable" gross amount as opposed to "net". Commissionable means the tour operator pays a commission to Anton Anderssen Travel for the booking. Net means the supplier pays nothing to Anton Anderssen for the booking. There is a difference between a "Travel Agent Discount" and a "Travel Agent Rate." If the price is practically free, then you can be sure it's a "Travel Agent Rate" or what we call a "FAM". That's OK to take. But if their "Travel Agent Discount" means they are cutting Anton Anderssen Travel out of receiving a commission (typically 5 - 10%) and handing it over to you the student, then no, that's not allowed. The travel agency relies on those commission payments to stay in business. You can always take what is called a FAM. For example, Universal Studios Vacations offers a FAM for travel agents for $99 including 4 days of hotel, 4 days of car, 3 days of admission to the theme parks, dinner at Hard Rock Café, and more. That's fine to take because the supplier never meant for the vacation to be offered to the public, with a commission. That's not the same thing as taking a normal fare offered to the public then cutting out the commission normally going to Anton Anderssen Travel and giving what would have been a commission as a discount to the student – that kind of thing is not allowed. When in doubt, ask the supplier point blank "Are you quoting me a price that is cutting the agency out of a commission and giving me that commission amount as a discount?"

Why would I want to work for Anton Anderssen Travel instead of just starting my own travel agency? Because it's free! Anton is letting you use his licenses, credentials, contracts, and affiliations. If you didn't use his, getting your own would cost you a fortune! To start your own agency, you need about $50,000 lying around the house to get started from scratch; or you could buy into a franchise. The largest home-based independent travel agent franchise company, TPI, charges $5000 franchise fee to sign up with them, plus require ticketing fees (see http://195.94.88.98/e2851183.html) There is a minimum investment of $10,000 with them, but you don't have to pay anything to be with Anton Anderssen Travel!

No one at the travel agencies in the malls would hire you as a travel agent without years of experience and without knowing how to write airline tickets on a CRS / GDS. Anton Anderssen Travel is willing to take you on without any experience.

Why is Anton Anderssen Travel promoting the CLIA card as opposed to other travel agent ID cards? The CLIA card gets you really great discounts without having to constantly prove your income every 12 months. The rules for getting it are easier, which is helpful to most new travel agents selling leisure packages to their friends. The CLIA card is associated with the cruise lines, and is one of the cards accepted by other suppliers like Alamo rent-a-car for travel agent rates. There are other types of cards, for example the IATA card. It's not issued by the cruise line organization, it's issued by the airlines organization. It's unrealistic that you can earn that card very quickly. First of all they audit your income (and many people don't like that). If you just sold published airfare, you could earn the IATA card if you could sell $250,000 worth of airfare every 12 months. That's over $20,000 a month in sales (and you have to prove it.) Most students don't want to work that hard, nor do they want to disclose their incomes to organizations every 12 months. The IATA card lets you take advantage of 75% off airfares (as long as it's full fare) but the sale fares offered by the airlines and internet specials tend to be cheaper than 75% off a full fare...therefore it's somewhat useless for most students to have an IATA card for airfares. Since we are a CLIA travel agency, we get cheaper travel agent rates on cruises than non-CLIA agencies...like $20 per day on select Princess cruises. That $20 per day covers your food, entertainment, accommodations, and activities on the ship. The CLIA card also offers fun discounts

How can I find the lowest published airfares between two cities? If you have flexibility, visit http://my.yahoo.com and edit "best fares".

Can I call up an airline and tell them I am a travel agent and I want them to book the flights, mail me the tickets, and give me credit as a travel agent? Usually NO. Airlines won't do the work for you (only tour packagers will do the work for you) (The only exceptions are Spirit, USA3000 and AirTran, and even then you must do it from the web site) If you want credit as a travel agent for directly booking flights with airlines, you have to buy sabre software, load it on your computer, pay $65 a month for sabre fees, pay $17 per ticket for ticketing fees, go to school to learn sabre, do an inquiry on sabre for the tickets, price out the tickets, store the fare, run the ticket, then bill a "booking fee" to the customer. In other words, if you want to get credit for booking fares offered directly from airlines, you have to do all of your own work (plus most airlines don't pay you). For most everyone who is a travel agent intern, it's not worth the hassle.

How can I get a toll-free number at a cheap price for my customers to contact me? You can get a toll free number from Anton Anderssen Travel Long Distance Services. Go to internet site http://LD.net/?antontravel and click on "long distance" Rates begin at 3.9 cents per minute for your toll free calls or any outbound long distance.

How can I get video tapes duplicated for clients? Call Media Sys 586 268 8260

Anton Anderssen Fan Club

http://groups.yahoo.com/group/Anton/

You can sign up for Anton's fan club to receive emails about Anton's upcoming special events, concerts, future classes, and more!

Anton's Travel Bargains

groups.yahoo.com/group/AntonTravel

You can sign up to receive travel bargain announcements sent to you via email from this site.

Don't Forget

You are never allowed to cut the commission out of a booking. If it's "NET", add 10%. If commission is built into the customer's vacation price ("COMMISSIONABLE"), make sure you remit payment to the supplier for the entire customer's price, not just the portion the agency is required to pay to the supplier. Failure to follow this rule constitutes fraud and theft. Likewise you can't book rates that are especially priced for travel agents to use for their personal travel until you earn your Travel Agent ID card. These rates are usually called FAM rates and they are super cheap but only offered to travel agents who have earned the right to enjoy that special price.

Thank you for purchasing a copy of this book. Here's a special offer for promotional copies of <u>Become a Vacation & Leisure Travel Agent</u> at a special price to give to your friends.

Send $15 per book, plus $2 flat rate for shipping regardless of the number of copies ordered. On your check's memo area write promotional code "Agent Special" and make check payable to Anton Anderssen. You will receive your book from the author's promotional printings, and therefore they could be very slightly different from this book (e.g. no bar code or price printed on the cover, etc.) Stock may be limited. Will ship whenever promotional copies become available. Mail to

> Anton Anderssen   4177 Garrick Ave
> Warren Mi 48091

Please do not make any shipping inquiries until you are certain your check has cleared your bank.

To join Anton's fan club, and hear about his latest news, see http://www.AntonAnderssen.com